PRIVATE L

The Fastest Way to FIND and BRAND Your Own Products and Make A TON of Money Selling on AMAZON

PRIVATE LABEL
U N I V E R S I T Y

This book includes the five-step process to private labeling products and launching a business on Amazon. The strategies, tips, and SECRETS you will learn from this book can be used RIGHT NOW to launch your own private label business.

NO EXPERIENCE REQUIRED!

Looking for a free quick start?

Join us at http://bit.ly/PLUbootcamp for our FREE five-day boot camp to private labeling.

For more information, contact info@privatelabeluniversity.com

Editor: Jennifer M. Barry

ISBN-13: 978-1975685317

ISBN-10: 1975685318

Acknowledgements

This book is dedicated to all the budding entrepreneurs who are not quite ready to release the "entrepreneur" inside them. The dream is on the other side. Follow your dream. – *Karen Gwartzman*

Without the example of my mentor, my father, I would not be who I am today. He encouraged me to carry out my entrepreneurial dreams and taught me to always be one step ahead. Many of the strategies and tips you will learn in this book were developed by him over 60 years ago while he built his private label empire. – *Neil Gwartzman*

To our incredible kids, Brynn and Brayden, follow YOUR DREAMS. Greatness is in your path. And always remember… To the Moon and Back…

To our families and friends, thank you for all the support and encouragement. See, every great dream begins with a dreamer.

Our hope is that, after reading this book, you will see opportunities everywhere. Opportunity is there, you just have to start listening a little harder. And when you do, BIG things will happen.

"There is nothing like a dream to create the future." –Victor Hugo, Les Miserables

Thank you and enjoy the read.

Karen and Neil

p.s. If you love this book and found value, please post a review on Amazon at http://amzn.to/2sr4oi3. If you don't like it, send us an email and tell us why and we will give you your money back. My direct email is Karen@privatelabeluniversity.com

Introduction

The Opportunity is REAL and Available to ANYONE!

So, here's the thing…

If you bought this book because you've heard that you'll wake up tomorrow a millionaire by selling products on Amazon, then close the book now. This book is *not* for you.

What you've heard is the noise and hype from marketers trying to sell you a product or a service based on a little knowledge they may have.

The fact is, the day after you read this book, you will not see $1,000,000 deposited in your bank account. The private label product business, just like all other businesses, does not work like that. Businesses need time to grow, and when they do, *amazing* results come with it. And yes, millions…

We're not marketers—just real people, like you. We work in the trenches every day, run four businesses, and spend much of our time teaching entrepreneurs and developing products for chain stores globally.

We work hard, but we play hard too. The private label physical product business model has allowed us to enjoy the riches of this industry. It has given us the wealth to be able to afford vacations on demand; beautiful, lavish things; and send our kids to the best private colleges. **Most importantly,** it has allowed us to work on our terms and have control of our lives. There is nothing more fulfilling than working and living on your terms!

We've been in this industry for over three decades. During that time, we've developed a powerful skillset that we share with like-minded entrepreneurs who are ready to jump into the entrepreneurial world and share their passion and brand globally.

A quick secret... The physical product industry is booming, and since the beginning of time it has been one of the most lucrative business models of all time. Think about it: How many times a day or week do you buy a product? Everyone needs and buys products. The person who has the products to sell are the ones making the money.

So, the big question...

Will you make millions? Many people—many of our clients, in fact—do make millions. And yes, this could be you. But it doesn't happen in a day.

So, here is our guarantee… In this book, we'll provide you with the five-step formula that will start you on the path to make millions. We'll make you laugh, touch emotions you didn't know you had, and at the same time give you a ton of nuggets of information that you've never heard before. The best part is, you'll be able to immediately apply all this information in your business. If you follow the steps in this book, you will be on the right path to success.

Private Label Secrets **was written with** the following entrepreneurs in mind. If you fall into one of these statements below, then this book is definitely, for you:

- Are you thinking about starting a business on Amazon, but you're not sure where to start?
- Are you a personal, business, or health coach looking to grow your brand and attract more clients?
- Do you run a service-based business and want more clients to know about your brand on a global scale?
- Do you have a retail business but have a hard time keeping up with the competition online?
- Do you want to leave your current job and you're looking for an exit plan?

No matter what brought you to the amazing world of private labeling, chances are you've spent considerable time searching online for information that can help you. You may have read a few books, perused countless blogs from the so-called "experts," or participated in webinars.

But how many times have you participated in a free online training or read through material that only made you more confused?

If this has happened to you, you're not alone. The vast majority of free trainings only give you bits and pieces of the larger puzzle, leaving you with an incomplete picture of how to make everything fit together into a profitable private label business.

This creates an exceedingly tough environment for innovative entrepreneurs to navigate what's legitimate and what's just too good to be true. These are some of the main reasons we wrote this book.

We want to remove the mystery and show everyday dreamers that creating a profitable business in this industry doesn't have to be a confusing, frustrating process.

This book contains the tips, tricks, and hidden secrets of product sourcing, manufacturing, importing, and sales that we've spent the last thirty-five years perfecting in our own private label businesses.

We won't just pass along a few pieces of the puzzle to get you going in the right direction; this book will give you *all* the secrets you'll need to start a successful private label business so that you can start making the income you deserve.

Private labeling is for ANYONE! Literally.

Private labeling offers exceptional opportunities to transform your career, income, and personal life. Over the years, we've watched people from all walks of life find incredible success in this industry.

We've seen real estate agents use private labeling to build their personal brand and bring in more business. We've mentored stay-at-home moms and dads looking to boost their monthly household income, young professionals who don't want to become a cog in the corporate machine, and retirees who view their retirement as an opportunity to try something new.

We've watched countless service-oriented businesses add private label products to their current product line to boost brand awareness and annual profits. We've worked with business, heath, and personal coaches who use private labeling to deepen their personal brand and create a wider client base.

Take Tracy, one of our former PLU students, as an example. A truly gifted health coach, Tracy had years of experience teaching people about nutrition, diet, and holistic health. She was looking for new ways to grow her personal brand and bring in more business, so she joined us on our annual trip to the Canton Fair in Guangzhou, China.

Like all of the PLU students who attend the Canton Fair with us, Tracy experienced 100% success and found a perfect product for her business. She private labeled the product to fit her brand and brought it home to her clients.

Her clients loved what the product did for their health and word spread quickly. Not only did Tracy add forty-two clients to her health coaching business in two short months, but she is also now making a residual monthly income by selling her product on Amazon.

Imagine what an extra forty-two new clients could do for your business. And that was in two months. What would that look like for you in twelve months? Monthly income and a *ton* more clients.

Benefits of Private Labeling

We can confidently say that the advantages private labeling offers are far-reaching and have the potential to transform your entire life. When you private label:

- You gain the opportunity to build brand recognition and brand loyalty on a global scale because private labeling allows you to personalize the customer's experience. Your brand becomes an identity, which will propel marketing and customer loyalty to your product. Starbucks is a perfect example of a company who has built incredible brand recognition and brand loyalty with a simple, everyday product.
- Everything is custom tailored to your product. The way it's shipped, labeled, and packaged, even the specific experience your customers have when opening the box is something you can customize.

- A unique opportunity to **control** things throughout the process, like marketing, pricing, sales distribution, and of course, all of your profits become yours.
- Finally, attracting customers to your brand will widen the scope of reach. Who doesn't want more customers?

Private labeling gives you the opportunity to make your business *exactly* what you want it to be, and you'll get to position your product line in a way that allows it to grow exponentially. You'll also enjoy how much private labeling will teach you about business, trade, and the global economy.

Just think: Companies like Coca-Cola and Nike have totally shaped economies and cultures around the world. Isn't it amazing to realize that in their most basic form, those big companies are simply private label brands?

We truly believe in the power of authentic relationships.

We are strong believers in the power of transparency at the Private Label University®, which is why, throughout this book, you'll see us sharing openly about our background, beliefs, success stories and yes, even our family. We think that once you *really* know us, you'll be quick to realize we are the real deal. Instead of speaking fluff, we speak facts.

This book will give you everything you need to get started, and that may be enough for some of you. However, we know many of you want to dive in deep and gain access to *all* the tricks and strategies for success.

Many of you are scared to start. This is normal, so we want to give you access to the opportunity to follow along and gain the hand-holding guidance and support you need beyond this book.

We're not marketing our services and products in the book as this is a training and sharing book. We do, however, want to mention that, for those of you who want to jump right in full force and get access to the complete, in-depth training program (The Import Success Formula®) or work directly with us live in China or 1:1, we will show you how to access all that support and knowledge at the end of the book.

The "Think Big" Generation

We've always tried to teach our kids to find their sparkle and reach for the stars. Children truly are living proof that no matter your education level or age, anything is possible if you have a proven process to follow and belief in yourself.

We want to share with you an inspirational story about our fantastic son. He started his first private label business when he was just fourteen years old. He took an idea and built it from the ground up, and within eighty-two days, he had sourced and launched his private label brand. In his first seven days after launching on Amazon, he made over $1,500.

He had no experience in sourcing or importing, and although he had two savvy parents in the industry, we guided him on his private label path the same way we've guided our students. He took the steps you are about to learn, ignited his passion, and launched a successful business using the private label business model. The business skills he learned at fourteen through the process have given him invaluable tools that he'll continue to use to start many more businesses down the road. So, again we say, if a fourteen-year-old can do this, anyone is capable of making their dreams come true.

If you're reading this book, maybe you're a budding entrepreneur with big dreams. It doesn't matter your age, your education, or work experience; we all have the budding entrepreneur in us. Many of us don't release the entrepreneur in us but if you're here, you may be ready to.

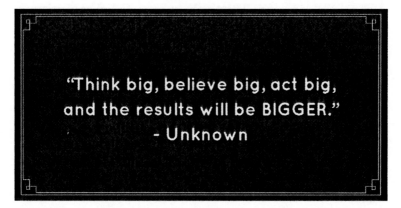

"Think big, believe big, act big, and the results will be BIGGER."
- Unknown

Get ready to be part of the **"think big" generation.** You're joining a vibrant community of individuals that have pushed back against the status quo in order to find a more fulfilling balance between purpose and success in life. We are so thrilled you are taking the leap with us — after all, we too are budding entrepreneurs.

And always remember: we don't ever want you struggling.

If any questions arise as you read this book, head over to our flourishing online community for 24/7 support and access to incredible resources to help you along the way.

Don't be shy in reaching out. We're here to help you grow!

Search for the Secrets...

Play the game with us and WIN.

We have so many secrets to share with you. Some are very personal, some are tragic, and still others are fun. Uncover the secrets throughout the book and collect the secret letters. Unscramble the secret word, and share with us over on our private site.

When you share with us that you cracked the "Private Label Secret" code, we'll give you entry into our monthly drawing of an Amazon gift card. Every month, we will draw a winner, and that winner could be you. (Hint: There are six letters in the book to find.)

Chapter 1

The Secret Sauce to Private Label Success - *The Unique Signature Formula*

If you've ever thought about starting a business, you've probably made a pros and cons list. The pros might include the many freedoms that come with being your own boss, like creating your own schedule, working from wherever you want, having more time to spend with family or friends, and the personal satisfaction that comes with building something out of nothing.

The cons, of course, involve the initial investment you'll make, both in time and money. You'll have to work hard to get your business off the ground, and that might require a bigger sacrifice than you anticipated.

Entrepreneurship is hard work, but in our experience, the benefits far outweigh the challenges. If you're worried about making mistakes, wondering where you'll find the cash to invest, or simply just trying to figure out where to start, we have great news: none of these challenges are too big to overcome.

Your big-picture vision, which we'll help you create in this chapter, will be the guiding force that carries you through all the highs and lows of being a business owner, and will be the core ingredient of your private label business. Yes, this is the secret sauce to product success.

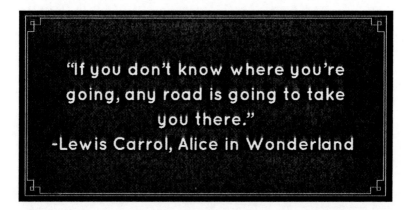

"If you don't know where you're going, any road is going to take you there."
-Lewis Carrol, Alice in Wonderland

Let's jump right in by outlining the Private Label University's tools to success: our Unique Signature Formula.

We will dive in deeper with examples a little later, but first, let's focus on the top three things most entrepreneurs either try to avoid or tend to forget.

1. Outline your goals.

Creating business goals begins with defining why you are here and where you are going. Here are four big-picture questions to get you started:

(1) Why are you reading this book right now?

(2) Where are you headed? What does life six months from now look like for you?

(3) Why are you going there? And what will you find there?

(4) What will happen when you reach that destination? How will your life be different?

(5) Who are you *really* doing this for?

Some of you reading this may be rolling your eyes. Don't underestimate the power of your big picture vision. As tempting as it may be to skim over these questions, your answers will provide the foundation for your business operations. Just humor us. Take a deeper look. Maybe you need answers to them more than you think.

Once you have a better sense for your vision, let's dig a little deeper. Take another five minutes to answer these more specific questions:

(1) What are your expectations for yourself in starting a business in the physical product industry?

(2) What kind of outside support are you looking for, and where are you going to find it?

(3) What does success mean to you? Remember: it means different things to different people.

(4) How many hours do you want to invest each week in your business?

We've helped launch thousands of physical product businesses over the last three decades. As serial entrepreneurs, we get it. Sometimes it's hard to sit down and really think through this stuff.

We are enthusiastic by nature, dreamers at heart, eager to see our ideas come to life, right? But your success doesn't depend on how quickly you can launch your company.

Success is rooted in an entrepreneur's ability to stay focused, disciplined, and on track with your vision.

These questions aren't just an exercise. They will be the fuel that keeps that Ferrari driving. We want to help you create a roadmap to success!

2. Keep your vision in front of you.

Once you identify your big "why" and "vision" for starting a business in the physical product industry, we strongly recommend that you put it in front of you.

Write it on an index card or Post-It Note. Put it somewhere visible in your office, above your desk, or on the bathroom mirror so it's the first thing you see every morning.

We are creatures of habit. If we don't see or do the same thing over and over, it just doesn't stick. Things can get misplaced. Good habits can be quickly forgotten.

Your future is not something you want misplaced or forgotten. So, go grab a pen and start writing.

3. Syncing your vision with your mindset.

Our mindset is informed by our beliefs, and beliefs are developed through life experience. In other words, your mindset is deeply rooted to your past experiences.

Why is this significant? Our mindset affects how we approach situations, how we interact with other people, and what decisions we make in life and business.

Just take Karen's story on the next page as an example.

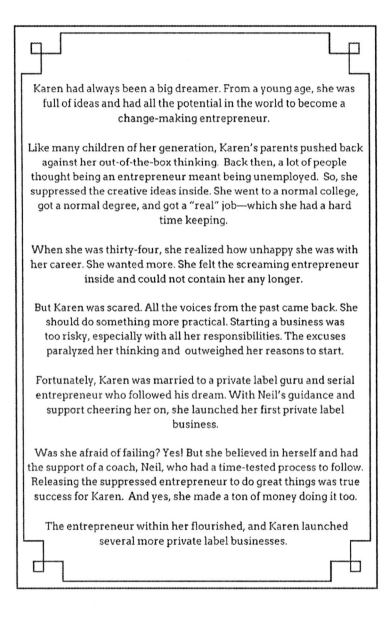

Karen had always been a big dreamer. From a young age, she was full of ideas and had all the potential in the world to become a change-making entrepreneur.

Like many children of her generation, Karen's parents pushed back against her out-of-the-box thinking. Back then, a lot of people thought being an entrepreneur meant being unemployed. So, she suppressed the creative ideas inside. She went to a normal college, got a normal degree, and got a "real" job—which she had a hard time keeping.

When she was thirty-four, she realized how unhappy she was with her career. She wanted more. She felt the screaming entrepreneur inside and could not contain her any longer.

But Karen was scared. All the voices from the past came back. She should do something more practical. Starting a business was too risky, especially with all her responsibilities. The excuses paralyzed her thinking and outweighed her reasons to start.

Fortunately, Karen was married to a private label guru and serial entrepreneur who followed his dream. With Neil's guidance and support cheering her on, she launched her first private label business.

Was she afraid of failing? Yes! But she believed in herself and had the support of a coach, Neil, who had a time-tested process to follow. Releasing the suppressed entrepreneur to do great things was true success for Karen. And yes, she made a ton of money doing it too.

The entrepreneur within her flourished, and Karen launched several more private label businesses.

Karen's story is a perfect example of how our mindset plays a crucial role during challenging times. Though her past tried to feed her fear and self-doubt, Karen was able to sync her mindset with her big-picture vision and has successfully launched a dozen private labeling businesses over the years. *You can only tame the tiger for so long.*

We've observed **three distinct ways** that mindset can impact how entrepreneurs make decisions. If you recognize them, they won't stand in the way of you reaching your greatest potential.

Fear — specifically the fear of failure.

What if I make a huge mistake along the way? What if no one is interested in this product? What if this is a dumb idea? The fear of failing is so normal. More often than not, failure gives us a priceless opportunity to learn something. In our experience, the journey of learning something new helped us better align with our vision. Failure has also made us better leaders, smarter decision-makers, and more innovative entrepreneurs.

Lack of confidence.

There always seems to be a small element of truth to our insecurity, right? That's part of its power. We've all struggled to find confidence at one time or another.

Have your thoughts ever challenged you or your decisions? Maybe you've thought: *There are lots of other people who could sell this product more efficiently than me. I'm not smart enough. I don't have what it takes to do this.*

It's true; there is a possibility you won't be able to do it. There probably *are* other people who are better, smarter, faster. But aren't you teachable? Disciplined? Don't you have the ability to learn, and with practice, become an expert?

Change your mindset by focusing on what you know. Become an expert at your trade/craft. Meditate on what you know to be true about yourself, your skill set, and your business acumen. Write these truths down and plaster them all over the place. You don't need to know everything, but you do need to know something. What is your something?

Misconception and Perception.

Have you ever experienced the exact situation with someone, only to leave the situation with a totally different conclusion? For example, expressing the desire to be an entrepreneur in the fifties, sixties, or even the eighties was frowned upon, and those entrepreneurs took a lot of grief when building their dreams. Many struggled and gave in to the notion of, "Well, I guess society is right: go get a real job."

But those who persevered and followed their dreams, did just that. Their perception of the situation they were in, had a totally different experience and mindset than those who quit. Imagine, entrepreneurs like Steve Jobs, Bill Gates, Richard Branson, Mark Zuckerberg, they changed the future. If they gave in to all the misconceptions and all the crazy insecure perceptions there would be no computers, no iPhones, no Facebook… Ugh. The power is now in the entrepreneur. They are the future.

We are the future.

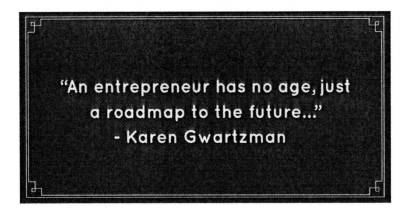

"An entrepreneur has no age, just a roadmap to the future..."
- Karen Gwartzman

In some ways, this mindset can be the most paralyzing. Our progressive, forward-thinking culture is still adjusting to the reality that being an entrepreneur is a real profession.

For a long time, having a "job" meant being a classified professional of some kind. Teacher. Factory Worker. Doctor. Mechanic. Secretary. Being an entrepreneur has no classification, which can lead many to misjudge (or flat-out misunderstand) the work you do.

The definition of a "job," according to Merriam-Webster, is "something that has to be done."

The issue with this definition are the words "has to." What if you have a job that you don't "have to" do, but you "want to" do? That is what being an entrepreneur is all about. It is about choosing what you "want to" do.

Listen, we get it: We *all* carry around a ton of baggage from our past experiences. Many times, these experiences stop us from doing and seeing greatness.

The thing is, we have choices. We have the choice to continue to have our past experiences control our tomorrow, or we can this day forward. We can take control, make our own choices, and create our own path for tomorrow.

PRIVATE LABEL SECRET #1

Bogged down by many of the fears mentioned above, it took Karen thirty-four years and eight jobs to realize that what she wanted all along was to release the entrepreneur inside her.

"Finally, I am happy, making better decisions, and doing what I LOVE and WANT to do." - Karen Gwartzman

{COLLECT LETTER P}

So, what is your mindset? Are you invigorated by challenges, or do you crumble when things don't go according to plan? Are you paralyzed by self-doubt, or do you zealously problem solve with out-of-the-box thinking? How will you maintain a success-oriented mindset in your early years of business?

This is why we're such strong proponents for defining your vision and goals before you launch your company. How will you ever fulfill your vision or reach your goals if your mindset isn't aligned with your beliefs?

Every entrepreneur would be well served to consider the three stumbling blocks above before launching their online selling business. Once you truly understand your why, your vision you will have the first insight to your personal Unique Signature.

Overview of the Unique Signature Formula®

Let's dive a little deeper into helping you understand your personal Unique Signature. If you're new to the industry, you've probably asked yourself questions such as, "How do I know what kind of products I should sell or add to my business?" or "How do I find the perfect product or category?"

Well, you are in luck.

We're going to share with you our proprietary Unique Signature Formula® that has helped entrepreneurs identify their core passions, vision, and purpose for creating a private label business. This formula has also helped find the right products to sell.

You heard it right: This formula will guide you to YOUR PERFECT PRODUCT.

If you're confused about where to start with brainstorming product ideas, just remember: The answer lies at the core of who you are.

Need some additional help? Head over to our website, PrivateLabelUniversity.com, and set up a call with our team. We'll help you brainstorm in the right direction.

Meet Yolanda.

She just fulfilled a life-long dream and purchased her first Ducati motorcycle. She has one last task to complete before she can ride: purchasing a helmet. A faithful Prime customer, Yolanda hops on Amazon to conduct her search. She finds two companies selling the best motorcycle helmet on the market.

The first company has a lower price, but no external website. When she clicks on their seller profile, she sees they also sell foam mattress toppers, specialty golf clubs, and a wide array of toys for toddlers.

The other company passionately shares their love of motorcycles. When describing the safety of their helmet, they use an inspirational video of a motorcycle cruising dreamy mountain roads. Their product description section is full of gorgeous pictures that explain the comfort and sleek design of the helmet. When she clicks on the seller profile, she sees dozens of other motorcycle products and accessories.

Which company do you think Yolanda will choose? Of course, the one that shows they know the motorcycle industry. The website content proves their credibility.

Which company would *you* choose?

The second company has clearly taken time to develop their Unique Signature; you see it in their **brand**.

After three decades in this industry, we've learned that people buy products based on feelings. Yolanda's story demonstrates how important it is to understand and know your Unique Signature.

Finding a way to appeal to your customers with your beliefs and passions is a critical step for every online entrepreneur. If you are not able to clearly communicate your passion, how will you convince customers to purchase your product? Your Unique Signature will help you:

1. Find the right product for YOU to sell.

2. Find a perfect niche.

3. Build a strong brand.

4. Attract customers that YOU WANT.

The formula is the key to your success. You will use this formula at every stage of company growth, from infancy to adulthood. Begin the journey toward finding your perfect product today!

Dive Right In: Identify Your Unique Signature

It's time to unlock the secrets to your online selling success. The following exercise will lead you to your Unique Signature.

Step 1: Answers the questions below. They can be answered as sentences or just words that come to mind. Step away for a few hours and revisit them again to see if you can add more.

Step 2: Take those same questions to three other people who are close to you. Ask them to think of you while answering the questions.

You want them to answer them as if they were you. It may feel odd to ask them to tell you about yourself, but doing this will open up a whole new vision for you. Start by saying, *"Based on what you know about me, how would you answer the following questions?"* Invite honesty! Write down their answers with a different colored pen or pencil for each person you ask.

Step 3: Once all the information is filled in, make note of the similarities between your answers and those of the people close to you.

Step 4: Take notice of what was said by the three people you asked. Were there words or sentences that they commented or mentioned that you did not mention or note when you asked yourself the questions? **Circle them**.

Why didn't you list or mention those qualities? Do they feel true to you?

Step 5: Take a deep breath and remove yourself from the exercise for a few minutes. Come back and look at all the circled words. This is the first step toward seeing amazing things about who you are and how others see you.

These words are not only what you believe is true about who you are as a person, but how others see you as well. They represent what you have to offer the world.

All this information that you just discovered about yourself will help you pick the perfect product, identify your niche, and bring your Unique Signature to all you do in business and in life.

This exercise is a wonderful tool you will keep coming back to when you need to align yourself with your true, Unique Signature.

Questions for the Unique Signature Formula

1. What are your special skills?

Look at all aspects of your life, as this will give you a better understanding of your Unique Signature. Consider:

• Family • Business/Technology • Sports/Hobbies • Certifications/Licenses

_____

_____

_____

_____

2. What education level, special schooling and/or certifications do you have?

_____

_____

_____

_____

3. What jobs and experiences have you had in the past?

_____

_____

_____

_____

4. What qualities do you have that make you unique?

For example, imaginative, kind, passionate, funny, empowering, ambitious, etc.

_____

_____

_____

_____

5. What kind of people do you like to hang around? Describe them.

_____

_____

_____

_____

6. What types of gifts do you like receiving?

_____

_____

_____

_____

7. If you could fix something in your home, what would it be?

_____

_____

_____

_____

8. What are you most passionate about? What drives you?

_____

_____

_____

_____

9. What activities do you like?

_____

_____

_____

_____

10. If you had a $100 gift card today to buy anything on Amazon, what would it be?

---

11. If you could invent something, what would it be?

Follow Up: Using Your Unique Signature Formula® (USF)

You have now generated some ideas about your core interests and passions. You've also invited several people who are close to you to confirm those findings. This is valuable information, and remember, it will help you pick the perfect product, identify your niche, and bring your Unique Signature to all you do in business and in life.

Think of ways that you can create a business around the themes that have surfaced, or ways that you can add those core passions to an already existing business. What product categories show up based on the results of the USF exercise? Health? Art? Beauty? Music? Pets? In Chapter 2, we will take your USF results and begin looking for the perfect products for your business.

Looking Ahead

Don't let your list of cons keep you from pursuing your dreams. Fear has a tendency to leave many budding entrepreneurs so paralyzed that they never end up starting their company. Just like anything in life, you control your success from this, or any other, course.

The remaining chapters will continue walking you through our proven five-step process to private labeling products and building a recognizable brand that will set you on the path to generating a healthy, continuous income.

We cannot guarantee that you'll be making a seven-figure income by the end of this book, but with the right combination of perseverance, patience, discipline, and mentoring you can and you will have the tools necessary to create a profitable business and lifestyle you control.

Now that you have your Unique Signature, let's take the next step and learn how to use it to find your perfect product. The world of online retail is full of opportunity. If you don't already have a product with your brand name on it, then keep reading because IT'S TIME TO GET ONE!

"Many people will tell you they made millions on Amazon and promise success 'the easy way.' The truth is that they have good marketing strategies but fail to deliver.

Neil And Karen have been in this industry for over 35 years. They are genuine. They've saved me (and helped me earn) hundreds of thousands of dollars, and I highly recommend them to anyone considering private labeling."
— Giles Fabris

Chapter 2

Your Perfect Product Is Right HERE...

Step #1 – Source, Source, and Source Until You Drop.

Selling physical products has always been one of the mainstays of commerce. After more than thirty-five years in this industry, we're convinced that finding a physical, shippable product to market and sell online has never been easier.

Just think: With the vast online marketplaces provided by Amazon, Ebay, Shopify, Etsy, and others, your product and brand has the potential to be viewed by millions of interested shoppers ready to buy, at any time of the day.

But where do you find the right product?

If you're reading this book, you probably already know that figuring out what to sell is one of the biggest challenges online entrepreneurs will face. It can be a grueling and time consuming process to find products, and in many cases this process usually leads to a very serious condition we call PPS. Perfect Product Syndrome®.

It's what we product entrepreneurs call Product Overwhelm. Perhaps you've already experienced symptoms of Perfect Product Syndrome®.

Do you suffer from Perfect Product Syndrome®?

Before we dive into the specifics of searching for the right product, we want to speak honestly about how this process can affect even the most seasoned private label veterans. Finding the right product to sell is time consuming, but it's one of the most important parts of a successful private label product business. Don't be surprised if takes you weeks, months, or even longer.

PRIVATE LABEL
SECRET #2

We have a LIGHTNING FAST way to find the perfect product and launch your business in less than five days. That's right; in just five days you can conquer the sourcing process and start making the killer income you deserve! And the best part? Every client who has followed our lightning fast sourcing route has enjoyed a 100% success rate! Take a sneak peek...

(COLLECT LETTER I)

Perfect Product Syndrome is a real source of frustration for entrepreneurs who struggle to source and sell products.

If you're spending too much time trying to find that perfect product, or spending too much money on an existing product that doesn't return a healthy profit margin, then you suffer from PPS.

In today's world of online marketing, sourcing, importing, and selling the perfect product has never been easier – or more profitable. And yet, we've seen PPS cripple the growth of businesses that should be successful.

If you haven't already experienced PPS, it will eventually surface. When it does, here are three things you can do about it.

Three Strategies for Preventing PPS

- **Remember to breathe.** Whether you're just launching a business or simply adding another product to your already thriving enterprise, there's no doubt that you will spend many long hours filtering through search results. All of this research will take a toll on you. When that moment hits— you know, that moment you feel your mind go into overdrive, completely overwhelmed by the millions of product options available—walk away for a bit. Go for a walk to recalibrate. I know it sounds simple, but taking a few minutes to breathe deeply has always worked wonders for us.

- **Revisit your big picture vision.** Remember all those Post-It Notes you put up after completing the goal-setting section at the beginning of this chapter? Reread those. Anchor yourself in the big-picture dreams you have for your life, business, and family.

- **Return to your Unique Signature Formula®.** Tap back into your passion. Turn your focus away from the millions of product options and center your attention on your specific niche. You've already done the hard work of honing in on what you want to sell. You may just need to remind yourself.

It is so easy, and very common, to lose focus while looking for products to sell. The longer you stay in the online selling business, the more you'll experience the cyclical nature of PPS. It will continue to surface, but with awareness and discipline, you can fight it.

Before we jump into finding the right product to private label, it's important to first discuss the different physical product business models.

Believe it or not, there are different types of products depending on the business model you are choose. Now you picked up this book because your focus is on Private Labeling. However, it is important to understand the other business models as it will give you added insight to the decisions you make in finding the right private label product and why.

So, let's briefly discuss what the physical product business models are…

Five Product Business Models for Selling Online: An Overview

(1) Manufacturing can be as simple as assembling a product in your home, or creating and building items in your garage. If you're a crafty DIY-er with a unique product that you create, this could be a great place to start. The benefit here, of course, is the opportunity for business growth that comes alongside the chance to save.

When the demand for your product reaches a point where you can no longer do it alone, you may choose to send your manufacturing overseas. You may also have the chance to buy raw materials in bulk, lowering your overall price to manufacture each item. These exciting changes will save you money while your business skyrockets.

(2) Drop shipping allows you to ship your products directly from the manufacturer to a storage facility, where they are kept safely by a third-party vendor until the point of sale. You simply create the website or seller account on

Ebay, Amazon, Shopify, Etsy, or any other online marketplace of your choice. When an order comes through, your vendor will package and ship the purchase to your customer. Perhaps the most widely recognized drop shipping service is offered to Amazon sellers, Fulfillment by Amazon (FBA).

Historically, drop shipping was a way for manufacturers to quickly get their product to consumers. For decades, this process was mediated by retailers. For example: If you needed a new washing machine, you would head to your local appliance store to check out new models.

Most of these mom-and-pop shops had a display floor and perhaps even ran an appliance repair business on the side, but very few housed inventory on site.

When customers placed an order, the retailer would send the order to the manufacturer. The manufacturer would then drop-ship the product directly from the factory to the customer's home.

Why does this matter to online sellers? When using drop shipping to send products to your customers, it can be easy to assume that the old rules of drop shipping apply. In other words, you might assume that the product is being sent directly from your supplier or manufacturer to your customer (or if you're in FBA, directly to an Amazon warehouse).

Here's the rub: Your inventory might make another stop along the way, which means more fees for your business. If your supplier says they will drop-ship the product for you, be sure to clarify *exactly* what they mean.

If they say they'll send your inventory to a "fulfillment center" via drop shipping, they're not necessarily talking about an FBA fulfillment center.

Many times, these "fulfillment centers" are simply separate warehouses that store inventory, and that's it. They are not true drop-shipping warehouses; your product cannot be sent directly to your customer.

Compare that to a true FBA fulfillment center, which holds your inventory until an order is placed, then packages and sends the product directly to your customer.

Remember: *"You sell it; we ship it"* is the heartbeat of drop shipping. All the handling, shipping, packaging, and fulfillment is handled for you, at a high cost. In fact, the whole point of this business model is that you don't have to lift a finger.

(3) Wholesale Arbitrage finds its sweet spot in large quantities. You don't necessarily need a website or even a warehouse (if using FBA). It does however, involve a large cash investment and, in some cases, high minimum order quantity (MOQ) In those cases, a warehouse will be needed. But—and this is so, so important—in order for this model to work, you will need the resources and/or connections to find suppliers, manufacturers, and distributors you can trust.

Sure, you can go on Alibaba or Ali Express and find a random wholesaler with a large product catalog. You could have hundreds of products at your disposal at the click of a button. But this is a short-term fix. If you're serious about long-term wholesaling, you will be better served selling wholesale direct from a manufacturer.

Just remember: It will take time to research the right product to sell and find the best wholesale source. More often than not, you'll build someone else's brand. Also, wholesaling sometimes involves contracts and MAP pricing, which will control your profit margins.

(4) Retail Arbitrage focuses on buying low and selling high. Sellers using retail arbitrage will purchase products at clearance prices and resell them online at a normal retail price. Places like Walmart and Target can be great options for buying low, but your competition will probably be greater because this is a *very* popular method chosen by online sellers.

Most sellers engaging in retail arbitrage buy in small quantities, at least initially, to test the product and see if it makes money. You won't be buying the season's best sellers off the shelf to resell; you'll shop the clearance section and barter for the best deals.

Retail arbitrage can be a great way to launch your business in the physical product industry, and many new online entrepreneurs use it when first figuring out how to source products. And don't get us wrong; there's nothing *technically* wrong with retail arbitrage. As long as you're careful, you can stay within the letter of the law.

But a quick word of caution. If you're looking to stay in this industry long term, retail arbitrage, wholesale arbitrage, and drop shipping are much riskier business models that leave you with less control of how much money you can actually make. Again, marketers have done a great job glorifying those physical product business models.

Take it from us, we have done *all* the physical product business models, and the most profitable is private labeling. Remember, the whole point of being an entrepreneur is to have more control of your business decisions and more control of your life. Private labeling will give you that!

Here are a few reasons why those business models lack possibilities for long term success:

Brand owners are fighting back. Target, Nike and more, for example, are just a few of the *thousands* of brands that are cracking down on resellers purchasing their products.

The ever growing list of restrictions on selling platforms. Because brands are fighting back, sellers will soon be required to be—or in many cases, already have to be—pre-approved by the owner of the brand. Sellers also must prove they are buying from authentic sources as a matter of course.

What's more, Amazon, Shopify, and others now demand a more careful assessment of product conditions. They don't consider items bought retail and resold to be new; they see them as used. And, as of Autumn 2016, Amazon accepts fewer receipts from sellers when a customer files an *inauthentic complaint*. In fact, Amazon has been leaning toward suspending the seller account entirely. Yikes!

How will you maintain your value proposition? There are thousands of retail arbitrage sellers looking to do the same thing you are. The competition is fierce and it can be difficult to keep creating unique value propositions to your customers when you sell the exact same product as everyone else.

At what point are you just competing on price? When you can no longer differentiate your value proposition from your competitors, the only thing left to compete on is price. And that's exactly how a majority businesses end up failing.

If you truly want to have a successful business, never set yourself up to compete on price. At the end of the day, it's very difficult to scale a business using retail arbitrage. Because this business model necessitates selling a wide variety of products to generate consistent sales month after month, you will constantly need to be adding new products.

How many stores will you be able to run to before your free time is maxed out? How long until you're exhausted by the non-stop shopping? Don't limit yourself. There are much better business models out there that have higher profit margins at a significantly lower risk than what retail arbitrage offers, which leads us to our final business model.

You are building someone else's brand and business. Isn't the whole point of being an entrepreneur is that you build *your* vision and not someone else's? When you take on someone else's brand to sell, you not only are working on building someone else's dream but you have no control of the product itself or the amount of profit you make from the sale. Many brands instill MAP pricing and control the product and how it is sold. That, to us, is having no control.

(5) Private labeling—Ah, the sweet spot to product control and success. *And, of course, why you are here...* Private labeling is the act of placing your own brand or label on a product that you have manufactured or purchased from a manufacturer. As a retail strategy, private labeling is not new. For years, big grocery stores have taken generic items, labeled them as their own, and set them on the shelf right next to products with household brand names.

But for independent online sellers, private labeling is about identifying a niche away from the main competitors. It's about trademarks and copyrights. It's about personalized packaging when you ship the product to your customers. It's about gaining total control of a product and what profits you make on it.

Private labeling may require a slightly higher upfront investment (with trademarks, etc.), but we have over thirty-five years of private labeling experience, and trust us: The payoff can be *huge*.

We believe that private labeling is the most viable, sustainable business model—one you can grow with over time. Some of the things we think you'll love most about private labeling include:

- You'll always have your products available for re-purchase from your supplier(s).
- You won't need to hunt down deals; you'll have a consistent and dependable product source to buy from again and again.
- You'll have more leverage to differentiate your products from other sellers.
- You'll have more free time to research and analyze new products in order to grow your business and generate more revenue.
- Because you get to choose the price of your product when you sell, you get to decide how much money you make. In other words, you control your profit margins.

- Most importantly, each of your products will have a brand that is a valuable asset to your business. Your brand(s) will create a higher sense of quality and value with your customers
- You'll create a brand product that can reach customers globally.
- You'll build a real, sustainable business around your personal unique signature brand, something you could sell to investors later if you were interested. This gives you a huge advantage in business.

These are just a few of the incredible bonuses and benefits of private labeling, but you already know all that, that is why you picked up this book. Private labeling is truly the easiest and most profitable physical product business model out there.

So, are you ready to start brainstorming about products? Let's develop ideas around the areas that will lead you to *your* perfect product.

Find a Winning Product with Six Brainstorming Strategies

1. NO PAIN, NO GAIN: Identify the Pain Point

Identifying the problem that your potential customer has—and then, of course, providing the solution—is a timeless approach to making sales.

Whirlpool, for example, has been in business for over one hundred years because most people dislike, or simply don't have time for, hand-washing dishes and clothes.

Apple thrives because they provide innovative, affordable solutions for our desire to connect with the rest of the world. How about the wide variety of companies that offer products that remove dog and cat hair on clothes, furniture, carpet? You get the idea.

Our point is this: There is power in the pain! Start by identifying the frustrating or confusing experiences people have in their day-to-day lives.

2. THE TICK FACTOR: Identify Customer Passions

Almost as good as, maybe even better than, solving a customer pain point is catering to customer passions. When customers are passionate about something, they will often spend more money. Golfers, for example, are notorious for spending thousands of dollars to lower their score by even one stroke. Lodge Cast Iron has all but dominated the domestic cast iron market because they proudly display "Made in the USA." Their primary customers are, of course, those who are passionate about buying locally manufactured products.

Because passionate customers are generally more involved in both the industry and the buying process, you will have the opportunity to cultivate a deep customer loyalty to your brand.

3. FORGET BEDHEAD: What Makes You Excited to Get Out of Bed?

We're not suggesting that you have to choose products that you're passionate about. We do, however, suggest that you tap into your passion and build your business model from that foundation. If you follow your passion, you'll already know what the product is supposed to do, and you'll be able to communicate your passion in an authentic way.

Choose a product you can talk about, improve, and be passionate about selling. In our experience, passion is contagious and always drives more sales.

Or you could focus on a product you have experience with, maybe something you've interacted with regularly at some point in your career.

Maybe you were a mechanic, or a plumber, or worked in the tech industry. Maybe you're a parent to young kids and are constantly thinking of things that would make your life easier. No matter what you choose, having industry experience is a huge asset when customers ask you questions.

Whatever it is, being able to tap into your passion everyday will help fuel you during the inevitable cycle of highs and lows that your business will encounter. Again, refer to the Unique Signature Formula® exercise and see it unveiled.

4. IT'S RIGHT IN YOUR BACKYARD: Can You Buy the Item Locally?

If your product is readily available locally, that may be one less reason for people to seek out your product online. For example, most people who want to buy a toilet plunger simply go to their local hardware store. If your product can be bought locally, how will you differentiate yourself and convince people to buy from you online? Can you offer a better selection? Lower price? Higher quality? Faster shipping?

5. HIPSTERS STAY AHEAD OF THE CURVE: Capitalize on Cultural Trends

Uber and Lyft. AirBnB, HomeAway, and VRBO. What do all of these companies have in common? They are all extremely successful businesses, yes, but they're successful largely because the founder saw a cultural trend and jumped on it. With innovation and ingenuity, these entrepreneurs launched businesses that continue to shape our culture.

Where do you start identifying trends? The customer! Get out and talk to people. Stay active on Twitter, Snapchat, Facebook, LinkedIn, and Pinterest to see what people are talking about. If you pay attention, you might be able to filter out a short-term fad from a long-term trend.

In our experience, the bigger the customer problem and the more widespread the frustration, the more likely a temporary social fad will turn into a long-term cultural trend. Identifying cultural trends is a huge part of product research, so we'll return to this topic shortly.

6. MAKE SOME NOISE: Identify the Competition

How does the competitive landscape look for your product or category? Are there no competitors, a few competitors, or many? Tons of competition doesn't necessarily mean you shouldn't join the ranks; it can actually indicate a huge market opportunity.

To stand out, you'll have to get creative with product marketing by answering the question, *"What makes my product different?"* How do you offer unique value to your customers? These questions will require a fair amount of research, but don't worry—we pass along a few tips for the easiest way to identify competition later in the product research section.

Product Research: It Really Is Worth Your Time

Finding the right product starts with research. Lots and lots of research. But the time you put into researching is worth its weight in gold because it helps you identify the following:

• **Profitability**. Will the product actually make you money?

• **Demand**. If you know where to look, it's relatively simple to determine if your product is competitive or if the market is over-saturated. We share a few of our favorite tools with you below.

• **Private Labeling**. Can you private label the product? Will you be able to find the manufacturer to ask that question?

• **Trademarks and patents**. Will you need one? Save yourself time, money, and frustration by looking into this *before* placing an order with a supplier.

• **Manufacturers**. Researching your product idea can also help you avoid a huge headache that, sadly, we've seen happen more than once. A new entrepreneur gets excited about a product and starts forming their entire business model around it, only to find out there isn't a manufacturer who will actually make it for them. Talk about a buzzkill.

These are just five of the *many* ways product research helps set you up for success. Now let's dive into a few specific ways you can answer those questions.

Use Your Unique Signature Formula®

Identifying which product you want to sell can be a daunting, time-consuming process. This is precisely why we created the Unique Signature Formula®. Your Unique Signature will give you a better idea of who your audience is and what category you should be selling in—for example, Beauty & Personal Care, or Clothing & Shoes, or Homemade, or Home & Kitchen.

Help ensure that your product is successful for your business and unlock your Unique Signature by following the USF exercise outlined in Chapter 1.

Conduct product research online.

Earlier, we discussed how researching cultural trends can be a great strategy for coming up with new product ideas. Let's talk more about that for a moment.

After using the Unique Signature Formula® to identify which product category you fall in, start checking out what's happening online. Here are two tools that have proven to be very useful for us:

(1) **Social media platforms.** Head over to Pinterest, YouTube, Reddit, Instagram and Snapchat. Even Facebook is a great place to start.

(2) **A simple Google search** for "trending products (year)" can yield incredible results.

Things to look for could include: What specific products are people talking about, commenting on, sharing, and "liking"? Which products are getting the most highly rated reviews? If you're in fashion, which new colors are coming into stores?

Best Seller Mentality: Think Like a WINNER

After identifying trending products and selecting a few that could interest you, head to an online selling platforms to see how those products are performing.

Spend time on Amazon, Ebay, Shopify, and others looking at the trending top sellers. Really take time to read through product pages and all product reviews. And don't skip the bad ones.

Negative reviews can actually help you pick out which issues need to be corrected if you decide to private label the same product. Here are the direct links to Best Sellers Lists that we check regularly:

- **Amazon's** best sellers are updated hourly https://www.amazon.com/Best-Sellers/zgbs

- **Ebay** regularly outlines what's new and hot on this page http://www.ebay.com/ctg

- **Shopify** keeps an updated list of which products are trending on their selling platform

Keywords Are Key. Maybe you've settled on a few products that could be a good fit for your business but can't decide which one to start with. If that's the case, don't miss Google's Keyword Tool, which tells you what people are looking at online. This tool can help you identify which Google Ads are ranking highest according to search terms.

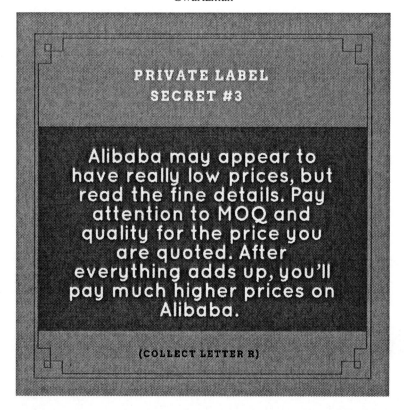

PRIVATE LABEL
SECRET #3

Alibaba may appear to have really low prices, but read the fine details. Pay attention to MOQ and quality for the price you are quoted. After everything adds up, you'll pay much higher prices on Alibaba.

(COLLECT LETTER R)

GET OFF THE COUCH: Product Research in Retail Stores and Trade Shows

If you've already spent several months researching products online without any success, you're probably itching to get out and hold, touch, feel actual products instead of just looking at pictures. Our favorite thing about product research in the real world is that it can work beautifully for pretty much every product category. Check out the trends in your local retail stores.

See what local tradeshows are going on in your area. We also strongly recommend reaching out to manufacturers of popular products to see if they would be willing to private label one of their products for you.

The Moleskine Experience...

Our experience with Moleskine is just one example of how working directly with manufacturers can be a great way to source products.

Moleskine has created a world-renowned brand with their reputable line of notebooks, sketchbooks, planners, address books, and journals.

Several years ago, we approached the Moleskine manufacturer and asked if they would be willing to private label a line of notebooks and journals for us. Since they also manufactured for Moleskine, we knew we would get a high quality, top-selling product that we could offer in our own online store as well as chain stores and independent boutiques across North America.

The result?

Our private labeled line of journals and notebooks are sold at a lower cost but with same attention to craftsmanship as Moleskine journals and, as such, have been a resounding success!

All that being said, don't be shy about reaching out to big name manufacturers that produce popular products. Sometimes this can be a great way to launch your first private label product.

You can also look for trade shows, which happen around the world all year long. To find them, simply search for an exhibition center near you and browse their upcoming events. You might need to provide a business card and contact details, but going to a show with a professional image gives suppliers a great impression of you.

The Fastest Way to Find Your Perfect Product

Find the newest products for the lowest prices in just three days.

Imagine a place bursting with energy and enthusiasm, where you constantly network with suppliers, manufacturers, and other buyers like yourself. A place where you can see, hold and test products that the rest of the world hasn't even seen yet. A place where you can be on the ground, in the trenches, building relationships with people that you'll do business with for decades to come. And doing all this in three days.

Amazingly, this place holds over sixty-thousand suppliers that offer the lowest prices *anywhere* in the world. By visiting this place, you gain direct access to hundreds of thousands of products from over sixty-thousand vendors, and the vast majority of these products haven't been released in the USA and Canada. That's right; having access to these products would give you the first crack at introducing them to the world.

This is a place we've been personally visiting twice a year since the late eighties. After three decades of private labeling success, we can confidently say that, if you want to find the newest products—and for the lowest prices—from reliable suppliers, *this* is the place to be!

We're talking, of course, about the Canton Trade Fair in Guangzhou, China. We've taken groups to this fair since the early nineties, and the results are *always* the same. A short week in Guangzhou is the quickest, most effective way to find real suppliers you can trust and a product that will provide a sustainable profit for the long haul. Learn more by visiting this website: http://bit.ly/PLUChina

When Neil first started going to this trade fair in the late eighties, no one was going. Back then, there was no Alibaba. There was no Amazon or Ebay. If you wanted to private label, you had to go to Asia to source products.

Some of the largest chain stores in the world hired Neil to show them what products to look for because they knew he was traveling to Asia all the time. Many of these products have been private labeled, and are now everyday items you see on the shelves of Walmart, Toys R Us, Michaels, LL Bean, and many more.

These days, supplier hubs like Alibaba or Ali Express can seem more convenient than a trip to China. But it's monumentally important to consider the whole picture before you put all your efforts into those sites.

Think about the time it will take to conduct online research—thousands and thousands of products to sort through. Time is money and if any one of you are like us, you want to see results and make money fast.

Even if you find something you're excited about, you'll have to rely on a picture. You'll have to trust that the quality of the product will reflect what is shown in the picture and description. And we can tell you first hand, it is never the same as the picture. Again, this will involve back and forth and time wasted.

Then of course, there's all the waiting. Communicating with suppliers online can take ages. Waiting for samples to arrive takes even longer. If you're pleased with the sample and place an order, you'll have to wait for that inventory to arrive before you can start selling.

Above all, you'll be placing your trust in complete strangers. Most people never interact face-to-face with their supplier on Alibaba or Ali Express. You'll send vast sums of money, without a middle man, and hope that your inventory arrives as planned.

So how do you access this incredible opportunity to attend the Canton Fair?

Join us on our next VIP LIVE China Event. We have discovered that the best way to see results is to not only learn the process but to implement it. We have put together a LIVE VIP EVENT for those who are ready to see 100% results. Our LIVE training prepares students for 100% success at the Canton Fair.

We train and implement all in one week. Our events are so popular and sell out because our students have 100% success finding products and suppliers, and receiving samples. And they do it within four days of attending the fair. Pretty bold statement right? But don't just take our word for it! You can check out some testimonials at http://bit.ly/PLUtestimonial.

These are from actual clients that attended the Canton Fair with us and had their lives and businesses transformed in just seven days.

The reason we have such huge success is we know the fair and we know how to do business in China. Not to mention, we have an incredible team that flies across the globe to support all our students. Yes, you get direct access and training personally from us, and you get our team or business partners and interpreters to guide you along the way. A little secret: Doing business in China is very different from doing business anywhere else in the world.

If you've been struggling to find the right place to source products from, or don't know how to find a supplier you can trust, the secret to your success could be waiting for you at the Canton Fair. Imagine: A week with the Private Label University in China will not only save you months and months of time and frustration, but will also give you a process, a team, and the support you need to be 100% successful in finding products and suppliers. To learn more about the benefits of attending this LIVE event in China, visit us at http://bit.ly/PLUChina.

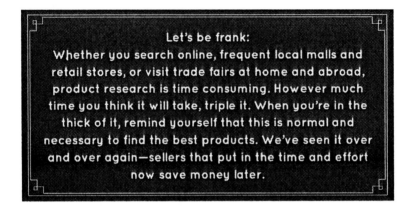

Let's be frank:
Whether you search online, frequent local malls and retail stores, or visit trade fairs at home and abroad, product research is time consuming. However much time you think it will take, triple it. When you're in the thick of it, remind yourself that this is normal and necessary to find the best products. We've seen it over and over again—sellers that put in the time and effort now save money later.

Terminology for Sourcing Products You Should Probably Know

While searching for products, especially if you're doing it online, it won't be long before you come across terms and acronyms you've never heard before.

Familiarizing yourself with them ahead of time can help ease your search. In fact, there will be industry-specific acronyms, terms, and descriptions used throughout this process, which is why we'll include a small dictionary of terms in each chapter.

You can also use the full Glossary of Terms & Acronyms at the end of this book.

Throughout the sourcing process, you're likely to come across the following:

ASIN: the number Amazon assigns to your product listing

ATOP: *At Time Of Posting.* We typically see this used in forums or Facebook groups when someone is getting the word out on a hot new deal, for example, *"ATOP I found this product for $8 each at Target."*

BB seller: *Buy Box Seller.* The person whose listing is shown when a customer is looking for products online.

BOLO: *Be On Look Out.* Many sellers use this for items that are sold out online but may still be available in stores locally.

BSR: *Best Sellers Rank.* Items on Amazon are ranked according to their sales volume and category.

Buy Box: the actual listing that a buyer sees of the product they want to purchase.

FBA – Fulfilled by Amazon

FBM – Fulfilled by Merchant

Gated category or **Restricted category:** products being sold on Amazon are monitored. Some categories, like healthcare & beauty, are restricted to ensure the health and safety of Amazon customers.

HBA: *Health & Beauty Aids.* Refers to a category on Amazon.

HTF: *Hard To Find.* These products often result in higher prices on Amazon.

IL: *Inventory Lab.* A popular company that offers inventory management and listing on Amazon.

Lightning deals: a promotion in which a limited number of discounts are offered on an item for a short period of time.

MOQ: *Minimum Order Quantity.* The smallest amount a supplier requires you to order. (Keep in mind we go into great depth in our teaching at our LIVE event how to negotiate like a pro.)

ProForma: An informal invoice that will outline what the intended purchase order will be.

SC: *Seller Central.* Your main dashboard when logged into your Amazon Seller Account.

Scouting: looking for products to resell online.

VC: Vendor Central

TIA: *Thanks In Advance.* You'll find this in online forums or discussion groups. When someone asks a question, they'll end with TIA, as if to say *thank you for any answers you may provide.*

Bonus Quick Tips

Researching Do's and Don'ts – quick tips when researching.

Time for a quick recap. When researching new product ideas, always be sure to assess:

- **Sales rank** of similar products on online selling platforms.
- **Product reviews**, especially taking note of negative reviews so you can improve on customer experience if you private label a similar product.
- **Competitive landscape** to see if the market is saturated with other people selling the exact same or similar product.
- The **price point** of sourcing the product. Do the math. What can you buy the product for and sell it for? Is there profit?
- What is the **size and weight** of the product? Will you incur huge shipping fees? What are the costs to store it at a third-party warehouse? Refer to Amazon's guidelines. Rule of thumb: If it is under two pounds and can fit in a bubble mailer or small box, you found an ideal product.
- Learn any **rules and regulations** for the product in your country.

At the same time, here's a list of products we strongly recommend avoiding, especially for first time sellers:

- Weapons of any kind
- Drugs or pharmaceuticals
- Wildlife
- Food products
- Brand name products
- Artisan products from other countries
- Any animal byproducts, especially elephant tusks and turtle shells

US Customs has been really cracking down in the last few years, and the importing process for these products is typically very tedious and expensive.

If you *are* interested in importing a product that falls into one of the categories above, make sure you

(1) contact Customs to make sure you fully understand the requirements you must fulfill, and

(2) research all local laws in your state, as specific states can have their own regulations on these types of products.

Understanding Gated Categories on Amazon

We bring up this topic now because we want to help you avoid unhappy surprises later on. As you consider which product you would like to sell, it's important to check if it falls into a gated category on Amazon. A gated, or restricted, category is simply a category or product that needs approval before you can start selling. If you do choose a gated category, that doesn't mean you can't sell that product on Amazon; it simply means you'll have to do a bit more paperwork to receive approval. Amazon restricts certain categories to protect customers. For example, skin care items in *Beauty* or supplements found in *Health & Personal Care*.

Every restricted category has different requirements and a unique process sellers must follow to "ungate" the category. Because there isn't a one-size-fits-all protocol to follow, the best advice we can offer is to visit Amazon's Categories and Products Requiring Approval page.

Our personal advice is to stay away from gated categories, especially if this is your first time selling on Amazon. Make the process easy and start making money before you jump into a category that may be harder to start selling in.

Before we move onto how to find a reliable supplier, we wanted to share Ava's story on the next page.

Ava's Success Story

Ava is an entrepreneur who wanted to start a private label business and launch it on Amazon. But her time was very limited. She's a full-time mom with a part-time job that she was hoping to leave. Ava was looking for a career transition, a career that she could have control of. She wanted to invest fifteen hours a week in building her business and not have to sacrifice time with her kids.

Ava decided to jump right into private labeling. She joined us in China for our LIVE training event. She was willing to make the investment in order to get started and see results as quickly as possible. She loved the idea of getting it all done in one week. It saved her time and money. She didn't have months to spend searching online; her time was worth so much more.

Her goal for attending the China live event was to start a private label business, leave her current part-time job, and work on her terms. With the training we provided before, during, and after the event, Ava was able to leave her job and is now working ten hours a week on her Amazon business, making more money than she has ever made in a "real job." And her start was all at our live event in China. The time she saved on the fast-track training in China got her product up and selling at a faster rate than if she sourced from home. Her brand is killing it in an international market, and she is reaching customers that she never would have had the opportunity to touch before.

"I saved a ton of time on sourcing, so I had more time to focus on getting my product in the hands of buyers, meaning more time spent making sales." – Ava L.

Wow, you did it! You are armed with the knowledge to find the Perfect Product. Now, it's time to find a supplier. The manufacturer who will brand your product with your label. We'll spend the next chapter outlining the step by step process you can follow to source products from suppliers you can trust.

Chapter 3

Suppliers Savvy

Step #2 – Your New Best Friend: Your Supplier

Congratulations! You've completed one of the hardest parts of launching a business in the physical product industry: deciding which product(s) you want to sell. Finding a supplier to source your product from, the next step of the process, can seem like an equally daunting process at first. Our goal in this chapter is to equip you with the tools you'll need to whittle down your options.

We'll demystify the various types of suppliers so you can determine which style is right for your business, and we'll outline the four most popular ways entrepreneurs search for suppliers.

You'll learn a few secrets to distinguish between suppliers you should stay away from and suppliers you can trust. We'll talk about how to order samples and, when you're ready, the five best ways to securely pay your supplier. We'll also pass along our list of terminology and acronyms that are widely used while communicating with a supplier.

Types of Suppliers

A **manufacturer** is the ultimate source of every supply chain, as they actually create the product at their factory. Working directly with manufacturers can offer incredible benefits, but keep in mind that some manufacturers don't have export licenses. If this happens, you'll have to work with an agent or trading company.

While buying directly from a manufacturer can offer a better deal, don't always assume you're getting the best price by buying direct. We've seen many product entrepreneurs get swindled by manufacturers who inflate prices because they know they're working with a foreigner who doesn't know better. The key is finding the right one to suit your needs.

Distributors have *exclusive* rights that allow them to import and sell a particular product in a certain country or region. Typically, products offered by a distributor are already part of their inventory. If you want to produce and deliver a small order urgently, and the order does not require much customization, sourcing from a distributor could be a great option.

Wholesalers are similar to trading companies; the main difference is that they (theoretically) carry inventory. Those who identify as wholesalers but do not carry inventory are actually traders. Wholesalers are in business to make a profit by buying from manufacturers, adding their margin, and reselling to you. Buying from wholesalers allows you to keep that margin.

Product offerings vary between wholesalers, and if you're buying inventory in bulk, this can be a cost-effective way to source your product. A genuine wholesaler will require your VAT or Tax ID number, which can help distinguish them from discount retailers and resellers who market, particularly online, as wholesalers.

Trading companies typically have long-standing relationships with other types of suppliers and buy products directly from them. They then trade the product to you for a fee.

Their income is from a margin they can obtain by buying from the manufacturer for less than they sell to you. The vast majority of suppliers on Alibaba are trading companies.

An **agent** is an individual who sources products from manufacturers, distributors, or other trading companies. Agents will typically sell any product, usually have little interest in the product itself, and will receive a commission on all sales. While you tend to get more personalized attention, you may never know exactly where the product comes from, as agents are not required to share that information with you.

There are no right or wrong supplier. You will need to decide which type of supplier is right for your business. However, keep in mind the more people involved or in contact with your product, the more fees and costs are added to the product cost.

For example, using an agent will inflate the price of a product, as they buy from a trading company, who buys from the manufacturer.

Determining Which Type of Supplier is Right for You

Deciding where you'll source your product from will be one of the most important decisions you make as you prepare your business for long-term success. Here are some questions to help you make the right pick:

- **Where will you get the best pricing?** Think beyond the price of the inventory. Include any fees for packaging, shipping, exporting or importing, duties, and customs as you negotiate with suppliers.

- **Who can provide the most reliable service?** Consider all of the following: How quickly does the supplier reply to your emails? Do they have English-speaking staff? Can you find any reviews from other buyers? How familiar are they with the specific product you're sourcing? In other words, how much experience does this supplier have with exporting and shipping your product?
- **Who is able to best provide you with a consistent supply of the product?** Don't work with a supplier that has a history of running out of inventory. This may seem like an obvious point, but you'd be surprised how many sellers run into this problem.
- **Who offers thorough product inspection prior to shipping?** Will they check to make sure the shipment is perfect every single time? The arrival of an imperfect shipment is one headache you don't want to worry about. If your supplier does their job well, it's a bridge you'll never have to cross. *(Note: Always do an inspection don't just rely on the supplier. We will discuss this in more detail later)*
- **What warranties and guarantees are offered?** If there is a problem with the product, will your supplier be able to repay or refund you? For example, if you're working with an agent or trading company, they may get your product from another supplier. This doesn't necessarily mean you should avoid sourcing products with them. Just be sure to check what kind of warranty or guarantee they offer if something goes wrong with whomever they source the product from.

Terminology Used While Communicating with Suppliers

Familiarizing yourself with the various terms, acronyms, and descriptions used while communicating with suppliers can feel like learning a new language. The following will help you get off to a good start.

CFR or C&F: *Cost and Freight.* A quote that does *not* include insurance. The supplier's liability ends once the goods are delivered to the carrier, whether by sea or air.

CIF: *Cost Insurance and Freight.* The quoted cost of door-to-door delivery, from the factory or warehouse of your supplier to you, and this particular quote includes insurance.

COGS: *Cost Of Goods Sold.*

Customs Broker: handles the importing of your product.

EX Works: outlines the price of purchasing a product directly from the factory. Any shipping fees or duties are typically not included in this quote.

FBM or **MFN**: *Fulfillment by Merchant* or *Merchant Fulfilled Network.* The merchant is responsible for picking, packing, and shipping the products, as well as providing customer support for the product.

FITCA: *Federal Import Trade Compliance Agency.*

Freight Agent: moves your freight around, either to you or another supplier.

FOB: *Freight On Board* or *Free on Board.* All freight charges to the point of loading have been included in the quoted price. If you receive an *FOB*, ask what freight and other charges will be involved in transporting your shipment to the air/sea port.

MAP: *Minimum Advertised Price.* A price agreement between suppliers and retailers stating the lowest price for an item to be advertised. Relevant when buying wholesale or direct from a manufacturer.

MOQ: *Minimum Order Quantity.*

Pro Forma Invoice: an invoice that confirms all the specifications of your order, sent to you by the supplier before you officially place the order. Not the same as a commercial invoice, which you'll need to ask for separately to ensure your shipment clears customs.

Replen: refers to an item that can be replenished, an item that can be purchased and sold repeatedly, usually from the same supplier.

Taxes, Tariffs, and Duties: additional charges related to importing. You'll need to have a clear understanding of what tax and tariff categories your product falls under, as well as any duties you owe to import it.

Alright, you have the lingo down now. Let's start searching for the "perfect" supplier.

Strategic Supplier Tips

There are a number of ways you can connect with suppliers, and some of these ways will expose you to suppliers who are more reputable than others. Here are the four most common ways product entrepreneurs find a supplier:

1. Searching Online

By far the most popular option, searching online can expose you to hundreds of reliable suppliers. The trick is knowing which suppliers and websites you can trust. Here are a few of our favorites:

• **Alibaba** has a gargantuan selection of vendors, but you will find a mixed bag in terms of quality and legitimacy. Alibaba's verification process sometimes involves an onsite inspection that proves that the business is registered and exists at the location stated.

Take this information with a grain of salt. Most of the verification processes involve only searching for a domain name online. Unfortunately, this does not establish that sellers are trustworthy and legit.

Always do your due diligence on every company before you make a large purchase, especially when trusting any supplier online. Remember, you have no idea who is on the other side of the computer.

Because Alibaba is so popular, we spend a whole section outlining how to navigate the suppliers on this site in our online training course, the Import Success Formula. Here is the link: http://www.importsuccessformula.com/program/. If you're serious about using Alibaba, make sure you tap into that resource.

• **Global Sources** uses a system almost identical to Alibaba. Their verification process also only covers whether or not they are a business appropriately registered with government authorities. Registration as a business is no guarantee of ethical behavior or reliability.

Even so, Global Sources and Alibaba are two of the more accessible options for product sourcing, especially for new sellers who are not ready to jump in and access China manufacturers directly.

• **HKTDC.com** thoroughly screens all of their verified suppliers. They have a smaller number of suppliers and higher prices, but a highly reputable verification and reporting system. As this is the official website of the Hong Kong Trade Development Council, it's unlikely any verified suppliers will risk their good standing with HKTDC by treating you unethically. As a general rule, look for suppliers that have been advertising with HKTDC for at least two years.

• **Made-in-China, Salehoo, TheTrader.co.uk and the Indian Handicraft Gift Fair** are a few of our other favorites. When you're searching these sites, remember that some verification symbols may have different meanings for each site, but it should be fairly easy to familiarize yourself with them.

2. Visit a Local Trade Exhibition

Local exhibitions provide opportunities to connect face to face with domestic and international suppliers. Product prices will be higher than at international trade fairs, but you can at least get a sense for how it feels to meet suppliers, test products, and enjoy the natural energy of a trade fair.

These shows happen year round, and they're easy to find. Search for an exhibition center near you and browse their upcoming events. Conduct a quick online search for "trade show or trade fair in {your city name}." Tsnn.com is another great resource for finding exhibitions. You may need time to sort through all the search results, but eventually you will find shows where products of interest to you are showcased.

Depending on where you live, you may need to travel to a bigger city for the best shows.

3. Overseas Trip to an International Trade Fair

Shh... This is the secret to finding the best prices and suppliers!

Face-to-face communication is of the utmost importance in Eastern cultures. If you source products from an overseas supplier, we strongly recommend budgeting for a trip to China, Vietnam, or wherever your supplier is located.

Organize your trip so it coincides with an international trade fair, like an exhibition hosted by HKTDC in Hong Kong or the Canton Fair in Guangzhou, China. There are also a number of trade shows in Europe.

If you're in a specific industry, like electronics, machinery, commodities, jewelry or textiles, make sure you search for industry-specific trade fairs. Like we discussed in Chapter 2, attending an international trade fair is the experience of a lifetime!

My dearest friend and mentor, Zhou, taught me the ins and outs of doing business in China. We met in the early nineties at the Canton Fair, and our friendship is still strong to this day. The strategies and skills he shared with me have allowed me to continue business with my factories and manufacturers for decades.

The biggest secret to success is taking action and going directly to the source. I have been attending fairs in China for decades and have had success 100% of the time. I've found new products that have not hit the market, incredibly low prices, and trustworthy suppliers that have supported my company and grown with me for decades.

Personally, when I look for products and suppliers, I don't search online sites. It takes too long. Instead, I go to China and invest one week in finding products and suppliers so I can start building brands.

Neil Gwartzman

4. Let the Private Label University Help You

Take advantage of our resources and training. We created a step-by-step process to suit all your needs.

1. The Import Success Formula – You'll find more than fifty videos to walk you through the step-by-step process of private labeling and launching on Amazon. We hold your hand through online videos and live events on our private community Facebook page.

2. The China Live event – Gives you everything you need: direct access to *us*, all the training you need to private label with success, and of course the VIP Canton Fair experience of a lifetime. During the trip, you'll receive training in the classroom, the factory, and directly in the fair. 100% success. Yes, this is the fastest way to find a product and supplier, and our favorite way.

3. PLU for-hire service that finds suppliers for you – Shoot us a quick message to learn more about what this entails.

4. Private 1:1 coaching. – This is available by appointment only.

So, you found a supplier that may be right for you. What happens next?

Your First Contact with a Supplier – What should you say?

Once you've found some potential suppliers who sell your products for the right price, it's time to send them an email or set up a call on Skype or WeChat. Kakao Talk and WhatsApp are two other popular calling and texting apps for international communication.

You may also have the privilege of meeting a potential supplier in person at a trade show, like the Canton Fair.

When you're first getting to know a supplier, there are a few important things you should share with them, as well as questions you should ask. Make sure you clarify:

- Your company name, title, and contact info
- Clarify the specific details about the product – if you found them online, use the listing
- Details on packaging, like quantity per case, weight of the item plus the carton, if an inner box is used, what marking is on the case, and use of pre-printed boxes
- Additional product photos
- A spreadsheet of all the items they offer/manufacture just in case they carry something else you're interested in
- Certifications, like ISO or ROHR or UL approvals
- Information about patents or trademarks on the product
- Their experience sending the product to your country
- Any private labeling opportunities for the product
- Which annual holidays the supplier observes, as it's important for you to know when they will be closed

Whether through email, phone, Skype, or in person at a trade fair, the first time you approach a supplier, use the time to gather information about them. Your focus should be on making a good impression and building a relationship. Don't tell them you're an online retailer, and don't exaggerate how much you're going to order. And whatever you do, never jump into bargaining right away.

Once you've gathered all the information you need to start doing business with them, you'll be ready to order samples.

Ordering Samples of the Product – It's not always about FREE

When you've shown a supplier that you're an expert in your respective product category, and that you're seriously interested in what they export, it's time to test their product.

Sometimes the supplier will ask you to pay for shipping for your sample and not the sample itself, which serves two purposes. First, it shows that your inquiry is a genuine commercial one. Second, they expect you to quote your shipping account number, which proves that you are in fact *in business*.

If the supplier is strict about not sending you free samples, you may just have to swallow the cost. Unfortunately, many overseas suppliers are constantly bombarded by people hoping to get a freebie.

This can make companies wary. Some will charge for samples, usually with a clause that if you order a commercial quantity, they will deduct the cost of the sample. If they do not suggest that, you could ask them to do so before you order your sample.

When the supplier quotes the total fee, including shipping and customs charges, check the math. Some suppliers will try to make a big profit by overcharging for the freight, which you can avoid by understanding the shipping rates yourself.

Another approach would be to either choose a small range of their products and place a sample order, or place a sample order for a few hundred dollars' worth of the particular item that interests you. They might prepay freight, and you may be pleasantly surprised to receive some sellable items for little more money than a single sample plus freight would have cost you. When doing this, be sure you make it *very* clear that this is a sample order to enable you to evaluate the product.

Dissect the Samples – This is the Fun Part!

Once you've received product samples, take time to examine the details. For example:

Material: Does it feel like a quality product, or does it feel cheap? Will you be able to truthfully market the quality of the product in your own online listing?

True to the photos: How does the product compare to the pictures the supplier originally sent you or product photos from the online listing?

Packaging: How did it arrive? Was it wrapped in a poly bag and thrown in a box, or was there more attention to detail? Ask the supplier if this is the exact way the product will be shipped to you. Keep this in mind when negotiating your own packaging and labeling.

Shipping time: How long did it take the product to reach you? Was it shorter/longer than promised? Ask if this will be the typical shipping time if you place a full order.

If you ordered more than one sample: Ensure the details are consistent in all the samples. Do they all appear to be exactly the same? What is different?

Your sample was PERFECT. Let's place an order with the supplier.

Your final order should give exact details regarding quantity, quality, price, freight method, freight terms, dispatch date, and any specific requirements such as packaging, weight, colors, size, etc.

If you use email to communicate with your supplier, set your email order to require a receipt. It's also important to specify that the supplier must notify you upon dispatch of the shipment.

Shortly after placing the order, your supplier will send you a pro forma invoice. In practice, a pro forma invoice functions as a sales agreement and no other form of agreement is necessary.

Once you receive it, make sure that all the details you've previously agreed upon are in order, such as price, dispatch date, freight method, and payment terms. Carefully confirm the order in writing using fax or email. Your supplier will then return a written confirmation, which may come in the form of a revised pro forma invoice, which of course you should check thoroughly before arranging payment.

Afraid to send money overseas? Five ways to securely pay your supplier:

Once you're satisfied with the product and have negotiated all the details of your order, you'll be nearly ready to pay for your first shipment of inventory. But what is the best way to send your money overseas? This is a concern that affects all importers, so let's run through five ways you can securely and safely pay your supplier.

1. **Deliver it yourself.** If you have a large shipment or are trying to get your products imported within a certain timeframe, it might be worth your while to head overseas and personally deliver the payment. You'll not only be able to guarantee the safe arrival of your money, but you can also inspect the shipment to ensure that everything is in order. You'll also be given the invaluable opportunity to meet your supplier face to face. However tempting this option is, 99.9% do not do this.

2. **Obtain a Letter of Credit (LOC or L/C).** If a trip overseas isn't in the books, your next best option is to get an LOC from the bank. This guarantee provides a wonderful safeguard, insuring that your bank will release your money as soon as all the specifics of your order have been met. This option can be slightly more time consuming and expensive, but the guarantee that comes with the LOC is priceless.

3. **Complete a Wire Transfer.** As long as your bank is well known and set up to properly complete international wire transfers, your money should

arrive at your beneficiary's bank. The only problem? There is no guarantee that *their* bank will release the money immediately. If time is of the essence for your order, we strongly recommend one of the two options above.

4. **Try Western Union (WU).** We recently interviewed WU and were impressed by some of the changes they've made to their business. Put simply, they now work with both your bank *and* your beneficiary's bank to facilitate your payment. This will also be your cheapest option, as WU typically charges between $22-25 for a wire transfer of any size.

5. **PayPal or Payoneer.** We're seeing more and more overseas companies set up accounts on PayPal through an affiliate bank in North America. The tracking features and security offered by PayPal makes this an ideal option. However, most overseas companies have to pay a fee to receive your money. If PayPal is the route you want to take, you can always offer to add the fee amount to your invoice so your supplier doesn't incur the extra charge.

Generally speaking, these methods apply to large orders requiring big payments. If your payment is under $10,000, everything will likely go smoothly when using a simple wire transfer. At the time of making payment, you should also remind the supplier that you must have a commercial invoice to accompany the goods. Ask for a copy of the invoice via email or fax.

Payment No-No's

- Never send money to a destination other than the address you've been communicating with from the start.
- Never send money to a company with a different name than the one you've been in contact with, unless you have proof they are a part of the same business group.

- Never make a payment to a personal account. Always use the supplier's company name to avoid losing your money.

As we've mentioned, choosing a product to sell and finding a supplier you can trust form the bedrock of every successful business in this industry. If you've made it this far, take a deep breath and congratulate yourself. You're more than halfway there!

But don't relax quite yet. In the next few chapters, we'll cover the important aspects of private labeling products, the nuances of packaging and shipping, the how-to's of the exporting and importing process, and the preparations for a smooth experience with Customs. These processes are detail oriented, and we're excited to give you all the tools you need for success.

Chapter 4

First Impressions Really Matter...

Step #3: Packaging, Labeling, and The Law, Oh My...

You only get one chance to make a first impression, which is why we've dedicated an entire chapter to the nuances of product labeling and packaging.

These are first things your customers will notice when they open the shipping box, and the proper attention to detail has the potential to create a loyal fan who will rave about your company to everyone in their life.

These details give you the unique ability to persuade consumer emotions, build brand recognition and loyalty, and even boost sales organically. Let's dive right in!

Types of Packaging

There are myriad ways to package your product in preparation for shipping.

A few of the more common methods include:

Poly Bags are simple plastic bags that come in hundreds of different shapes and sizes. This is by far the cheapest packaging option.

Some have zip locks at the top, others have plastic headers for hanging on retail shelves, and some have a sticky fold-over section at the bottom to close off the bag.

These are a common choice for Amazon sellers but, keep in mind, not the most exciting unboxing experience for your customer.

Clam shells likewise come in a wide variety of shapes and sizes, and are more durable than poly bags.

Some come equipped with a hole for hanging on a shelf in retail stores. Others, called *graphic boxes*, have a space for a label above where the product is stored.

Inner boxes give an extra layer of protection to products.

When you—or a customer, if you use drop shipping or FBA—open the shipping box, you'll immediately see another, smaller box containing the product.

Some online sellers package products themselves, while others use a packaging service provided by the supplier. If you choose the latter, be aware that most suppliers use the cheapest packaging option (poly bags), unless you request otherwise.

Always check with your supplier to make sure, especially if you're not interested in poly bags. You can often arrange to have all your pre-printed barcodes placed directly on the packaging.

Above all, don't be shy about the investment involved. Some entrepreneurs try to cut corners with packaging — after all, it just goes in the trash, right?

Let's look at a real-world example from Neil's early business life where this thought is proved wrong.

Neil was experiencing tremendous success selling unique mannequins to chain stores around the world. He didn't pay much attention to the way the mannequins were packaged because sales were skyrocketing and, truth be told, the packaging wasn't great.

When he crunched the numbers, he learned it would only cost another $0.05 to increase the quality of the packaging. Because he was ordering tens of thousands of mannequins at a time, he decided the extra cost wasn't worth it, even at the five cents. One summer, he was doing a trade show and was approached by a representative from Michaels. They loved the mannequins, but ultimately refused to place an order. When Neil asked why, the rep simply replied, "Your packaging is crap. Change the packaging and we would reconsider."

Neil immediately realized the fallacy in his thinking. Even though packaging ultimately ended up in the trash, he was missing out on a huge opportunity with a reputable chain store. Not surprisingly, Neil paid the five cents per mannequin to upgrade the packaging and Michaels placed an enormous order.

You never know what opportunities you may be missing out on when you try to cut corners on packaging quality. If you're cheap upfront, you may end up losing money in the end. Time and time again, we've found that investing in packaging increases sales and ends up saving us money in the long run.

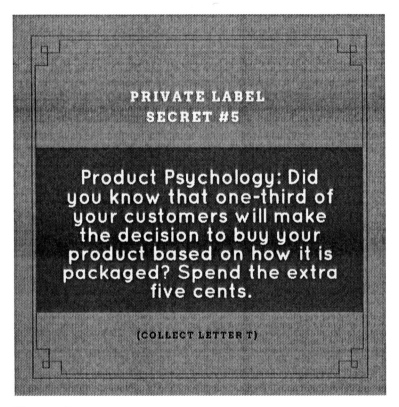

PRIVATE LABEL SECRET #5

Product Psychology: Did you know that one-third of your customers will make the decision to buy your product based on how it is packaged? Spend the extra five cents.

(COLLECT LETTER T)

Barcodes

Unfortunately, there is an incredible amount of misinformation out there about where and how to put barcodes on your products. Many companies suggest buying third-party barcodes. While they are cheap, they are not universally recognizable or even technically legal.

You must buy a legal, registered barcode that is unique to your product, and GS1 is the only company that provides this service globally. Putting a registered barcode on your products shows that you are a legitimate business and serious player in the physical product industry. Obtaining a barcode through GS1 is not too expensive, and it guarantees you will not run into any problems down the road.

Terminology for Packaging and Labeling

Some of the basic terms and acronyms you'll come across as you label and package your product.

ASIN: *Amazon Standard Identification Number.* This is given to every product you list on Amazon. Usually in the format B00xxxxxxx, an ASIN is attached to the listing, not the product itself. No two items will ever have the same ASIN. You can use this number when searching for a product on Amazon.

COO: *Country of Origin.* An important domestic regulation mandates that your product show the country where the it originated.

EAN: *European Article Number.* If you sell in Europe, your products will be assigned this thirteen-digit code, also called an International Article Number (IAN).

FNSKU: *Fulfillment Network Stock Keeping Unit.* These are the numbers printed directly on your product labels when you use FBA. FNSKUs identify your items so that the correct product is pulled for each sale.

GTIN: *Global Trade Identification Numbers.* These are universal identifiers used around the world to find product information across databases.

UPC: *Universal Product Code.* A twelve-digit barcode that can be found on almost all products in the retail world. This is also simply called the barcode.

WL: *White Labeling,* also referred to as *Private Labeling.* Involves purchasing an item from a manufacturer, applying your own brand, and reselling the product.

Packaging Inserts

Inserts are included inside the packaging to tell the consumer more about what they've purchased. Sometimes inserts include instructions for using or assembling the product. Inserts are a great way to build brand loyalty, as you can use inserts to share information about your company, your mission statement, any charities you're connected with, and of course, information about the product itself.

Inserts come in many forms. Pictures, brochures or handouts, CDs or DVDs, or even a pamphlet with a link to an app or website to further your customer's experience can be very useful.

We would especially recommend considering inserts if you are private labeling a product. Inserts provide a unique opportunity to tell your customers more of your story, create brand awareness, educate the buyer on the product, and, if it's done right, you can really boost the quality of the review a customer leaves you.

So, let's talk the LAW...

You are probably thinking, "What the heck is Legal doing in this packaging chapter?" Well, it absolutely belongs here, because what you write on your packaging, whether it is the copy, symbols such as a trademark, or a design, will need to stay in the confines of the law.

Firstly, let's talk about the product. It's important to remember that you do not own the product or its name until you have a patent or trademark for it.

If you choose not to take that route, the only thing you legally own is the private label and brand you have created. However, if that is not backed by the law, you open up an opportunity for someone else to claim it.

Many major manufacturers make a specific product for dozens, even hundreds, of different companies, and all those companies do not "own" the patent to the product.

Instead, they use the product and brand it with their legal mark.

Take any of your basic household products as an example. Whether it's toilet paper, paper towels, or tissues, these items are private labeled and branded by dozens of independent companies.

You know you've achieved ultimate private labeling success when your brand becomes the very name for the product itself, like Kleenex is to tissues, or Q-Tips is to cotton swabs. Neither Kleenex or Q-Tips own the rights to the specific products they sell; they've just created an incredible brand through decades of powerful marketing.

Trademarks or Patents: Are They Worth It?

Maybe you're not private labeling a generic product. You've found something unique at an international trade fair and you want exclusive rights to sell it in your country. Or perhaps you invented the product! This is *your* special, unique idea.

You've put an incredible amount of time, effort, and money into creating this product. The last thing you want is other people poaching off your hard work. The cost of protecting your idea is daunting—we get it. But the investment will be worth it in the long run.

If you're still a few years away from releasing the product to the public, start the patent work now. Even a simple *provisional patent* will give you time to test the item's profitability with consumers.

When should you file?

After your product has been tested, and after you've spoken with an attorney, you should feel confident to start the filing process.

Because of the upfront investment, many entrepreneurs decide to file for a patent or trademark specific to their country or continent. We understand that world patents and trademarks are expensive; just be sure to think it through.

If your product is only protected in the US, Canada, and Mexico, your manufacturer could lawfully sell your product throughout Europe, Asia, and elsewhere.

Beware of copyright issue

Be mindful when you are creating copy for your packaging and inserts, as well as any copy you might use for promotions, such as Amazon or social media.

You cannot make copyright claims, nor can you use terms like "patent pending" if, in fact, you never filed. Your claims must be real and backed with proof.

The same goes with any graphics and designs you use on your packaging. Make sure you obtain the right permissions and licensing prior to use.

A Few Considerations for the Private Label Process

Some of this might seem obvious, but let's run through some basic information to keep in mind as you private label your product.

Does the product already have a patent, trademark, or other type of license? Careful research will help ensure that you're not private labeling a product that has already been spoken for.

Don't assume that working with a manufacturer automatically means they're equipped to private label your product. If they don't have labeling and packaging equipment, they might be using other companies to fulfill your order.

Always over-communicate to ensure you're never left in the dark throughout your sourcing and importing journey.

Where on the product or package (or both) will you place the label? Some products require both. What exactly do you want the label to say or look like? What language(s) will you put on the label?

Check into the specific warning labels and safety regulation labels your product requires, which we talk more about next.

Where do all of your raw materials come from? Use this as a guide to determine how many countries need to be included on your Country of Origin label.

What color(s) and logo will you use to distinguish your brand? Is your company's contact information clearly displayed?

Warning Labels

Warning labels instruct the end user about risks associated with your product and may also include restrictions for certain uses of your product.

Requirements for warning labels vary by product category, but as a general rule, warning labels will be required for:

- Food products
- Electronic products
- Products that include anything sharp, flammable, or any risk of electric shock
- Products that should not be used by specific consumers. For example, *"Not suitable for children under the age of 3."*

Most toys require several risk warning labels and warnings about the use of magnets inside the toy. You'll also need to include safety regulations required for your product. *"Keep out of reach of children"* is the most common type of warning label in this category, but be sure to check what other labels your product requires.

Lastly, be sure to check with your shipping agent(s) and customs broker to see what warning labels you need for the shipping and importing process.

Determining the COO (Country of Origin) for Your Product

Customs requires all importers to clearly label their product's country of origin. Determining the country of origin can be tricky, so let's look at a few scenarios that use the US as an example:

- You've designed a product on US soil and export it overseas for manufacturing. The product is imported back to the US and packaged there before distribution.
- Your product is partially manufactured on US soil, and you export these materials to Vietnam to be assembled into the final product.
- The entire manufacturing and production process occurs in China, and you package the product on US soil before sending it to market.

What do all of these "country of origin" examples have in common? None of these products can legally use the label *Made in USA*. You could say "Made in China, Packaged in USA." You could even say "Designed in USA, Made in China." But if you claim your product was *Made in USA*, you run the risk of customs seizing your shipment, slapping on a hefty fine, and flagging your company.

If your product goes overseas at any point in the production process, it will require a COO label.

Criteria for Labels

Make sure all the labels meet the following criteria:

- All labels must be printed with permanent ink.
- All labels must be legible.
- Keep all warning labels, safety regulations, and certifications in one place on the packaging.
- Include all necessary COO labels.
- Keep a digital file of all labels your product requires.

We told you there would be a ton of details but fun. We always find when we teach this part of the process, it goes so quickly. The tons of info you receive makes total sense, plus it's fun.

You can be creative with the packaging to give your customer a better experience. So, now you're ready to turn your attention to shipping and importing your product. I know, it's not sexy... But wait! You may be in for a little surprise.

Chapter 5

Importing Made Sexy

Step# 4 – Import like the Pros

All right, so this chapter may not be very sexy, but this is *the step* that absolutely must be taken. If you don't do it, and know it, your products will never get into the hands of your customers. This means you won't make *any money.*

So, let's imagine something sexy and keep reading…

If the importing process feels daunting, we have good news: You're not alone. Most entrepreneurs find this part of the physical product industry overwhelming, and for good reason. There are myriad details that, if overlooked, can cause costly delays to your burgeoning business.

Remember: Any programs or individuals that tell you that you need a "degree in importing" or that you need to hire a company (maybe them!) to do the importing for you in order to be successful are wrong.

We were able to teach the steps involved to thousands and thousands of people through our online program, so implementation is easy and successful. You can do this.

In this chapter, we will dissect all the details involved in this part of the process so that, with careful study, you will discover how straightforward importing products can be.

Terminology for Importing & Shipping

Here are some common terms and acronyms you'll come across as you ship and import your inventory. Get ready to learn the importing and shipping jargon.

Anti-Dumping Tariff*: dumping occurs when a company exports a product at a price lower than the price it normally charges in its own home market. Anti-dumping tariffs are imposed by domestic government on foreign imports that it believes are priced below fair market value.

AWB: *Air Waybill.* A document used when shipping via air; ensures that the correct goods are delivered to you. The air waybill is provided by your airline or air freight forwarder. It acts as a receipt for your supplier, as it proves that your inventory has been sent.

Bill of Lading: similar to an AWB, this document is for sea freight and signifies that the goods described have been loaded on board the ship.

Bonds*: a contract that guarantees the payment of import duties and taxes.

Consignee: the owner or purchaser of the goods; the financially responsible party. Also referred to as the *Importer of Record.*

Deemed Value: an amount calculated by Customs in some countries to determine the value of the goods for duty & tax purposes.

FCL: *Full Container Load.* When your sea shipment fills a container.

FTL: *Full Truckload.* When your freight shipment fills an entire truck.

Freight Forwarder: facilitates the forwarding of shipments from the port to your receiving destination.

ISF: *Importer Security Filing.* A document that must be electronically submitted to Customs when your cargo is arriving into the US via sea freight.

LCL: *Less than Container Load.* When your sea shipment does not fill an entire container.

LTL: *Less than Truckload.* When your freight shipment does not fill an entire truck.

Schedule Rates: a rate chart published by the carrier. In the case of postal services, it is not subject to negotiation and you will always pay that rate. In the case of commercial carriers, it is the absolute maximum rate, which can usually be negotiated.

Tariff/Tariff Codes*: the taxes or duties to be paid on a particular class of imports or exports.

*an experienced customs broker (discussed below) will be an expert in these areas.

Holiday time - public Chinese holidays affect importing.

Before we jump into the nuanced details of the importing process, we want to encourage you to take a moment to review the major public holidays in each country that is connected to your supply chain.

Think about where your raw materials are sourced from and manufactured, where your supplier is located, and all ports your shipment will go through during the exporting process.

Remember that public holidays in other countries often look very different than our short three-day weekends here in North America. These holidays will affect the importing phase.

Let's use China as an example. When we shut down our businesses in North America, we announce it and the dates are set in stone. We close on the designated date and reopen when we say we will.

This is not always the case with Chinese companies. It's not uncommon for companies in China to close early, come back late, or both, and with no warning. Even if a factory sticks to the dates they give for their closure, their suppliers, distributors, or shipping couriers may not.

The reason is tied to local culture. During the year, Chinese workers live near their place of work and most of the time, the factory or shipping terminal is very far from their hometown—several days' worth of travel on a bus or train.

When Chinese New Year or Golden Week rolls around, they return to their family homes like we do during Thanksgiving and Christmas, with one big difference: many Chinese workers don't return to their jobs after a long holiday. Either they travel too far and take more time off or they just don't return.

As a result, many factory managers or shipping companies re-open with seriously depleted staff *and* a huge backlog of orders that were left at a standstill during the holiday. For you, this means one thing: DELAYS.

The massive human migration that occurs around Chinese holidays has taught us to add extra time before and after the actual holiday. For example, you should plan for halted production, reduced output, and severe shipping delays during the days or weeks before, during, and after the following:

- January: **New Year's Day**, three-day holiday > plan for **four to five days** of delays
- Jan/Feb: **Chinese New Year**, one-week holiday > plan for **three to four weeks** of delays
- April: **Qing Ming Festival**, three-day holiday > plan for **four to five** days
- May: **Labor Day**, one-day holiday > plan for **three days**
- May/June: **Dragon Boat Festival**, three-day holiday > plan for **four to five days**

- Sept/Oct: **Mid-Autumn Festival**, three-day holiday > plan for **five to six days**
- October: **Golden Week**, one-week holiday > plan for **two weeks** (or more if Golden Week overlaps with the mid-Autumn Festival)

In order to minimize the disruption to your business, plan ahead. While it may be difficult to book your orders in advance due to cash flow or warehouse space, the alternative is to frantically try to contact your supplier—who won't be checking their email—because your shelves are empty. The loss of sales that result from being out of stock for too long could be devastating for your business.

Or you may have to arrange a last-minute air freight shipment that breaks the bank because both air and sea freight rates are always inflated during major holidays.

Through careful forecasting and early buying, you should be able to bypass the problems caused by the backlog of orders Chinese companies receive, as well as the slow start faced when large numbers of employees do not return after the holiday.

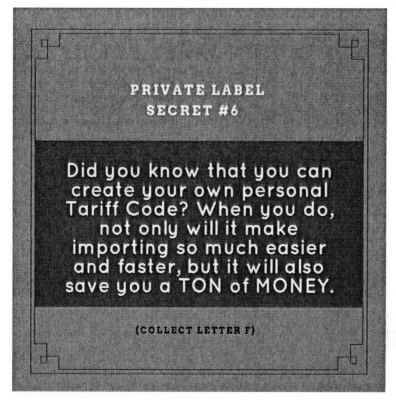

**PRIVATE LABEL
SECRET #6**

Did you know that you can create your own personal Tariff Code? When you do, not only will it make importing so much easier and faster, but it will also save you a TON of MONEY.

(COLLECT LETTER F)

Preparing Your Shipment for Customs

The first step when importing a product is to get connected with a Customs broker. But before you start interviewing brokers, take some time to do your own research:

1. Know your product classification.

Don't rely solely on your supplier or broker to know the nuances of tariff code classifications for you. As the importer, it's up to you to know exactly how your product should be classified.

Taking the time to thoroughly understand this for yourself could actually save you money. By really honing in on which tax codes apply to your product, you can avoid paying more than you need to—and who knows? Maybe you'll find your product actually falls under the "duty free" classification.

2. Utilize free resources.

Customs websites provide a great deal of helpful information, and they are free of charge. For example, you can get an idea of what duty rates you'll be paying with the Duty Calculator. Of course, if you want guaranteed accuracy, you'll need to contact an official customs office.

3. Interview licensed customs brokers.

A smooth importing process all comes down to being aligned with the right people. Because of this, interviewing customs brokers is not an uncommon occurrence. Customs brokers will be local to your area, and like we said, a simple online search usually yields enough results to get you started.

4. Investigate your logistic company's broker.

If you're working with a logistics company, start asking similar questions about their broker right away. Make sure you connect with that person, and if you don't think they're a good fit, let the company know you will be using a different broker. Then, initiate the interview process discussed above.

Importing costs: How much will I really have to pay?

Naturally, the exact importing costs you'll encounter depend on your specific product. Even still, let's look at an example of how importing costs can play out.

Let's say you find a low-priced product, and you determine that it will cost you $3 to get each item "landed" at your door—which includes the original price of the product, packaging and labeling, freight or shipping, customs, duty and taxes, insurance, currency conversion, and anything else. You decide to purchase enough inventory to cover the sale of one product per day for an entire year (365 days). With a low-cost landed price of $3, your upfront product investment will be $1,095.

The key is to make sure when you are calculating the cost of your item you are including all your expenses.

Of course, it's very likely you will be selling more than one product per day. Because you don't want to run out of inventory and run the risk of losing customers, your initial product investment may be much higher than our example here.

Also remember we're strictly talking about the cost of importing. There will still be many costs to pay after your inventory arrives, such as marketing, listing products on online marketplaces, storage fees, and others.

How does the product get shipped to me?

Your freight forwarder will help you arrange your shipment so that it leaves your supplier and shipped to you or the location of choice, like an Amazon warehouse.

If your first shipment is a smaller order, air freight could be a better and quicker option than sea freight.

If you're dealing with a larger shipment, and you don't need it ASAP, you'll have several freight options to consider:

- **Air Freight** is worth considering when you're concerned about the speed of delivery or, as we mentioned, when dealing with smaller orders. If you work with an air courier, your supplier will usually give you a door-to-door quote.

  If you use air freight, you'll receive an airport-to-airport quote. As always, look through the quote with a fine-tooth comb to ensure that *all* costs are listed.

- **Sea Freight** is a good option when you have a large-volume shipment and can afford to wait to receive your goods.

  If your order fills a container, it will be referred to as a Full Container Load (FCL). If it is less, it will be deemed Less than Container Load (LCL).

It's easy to think that the lowest freight cost per item is the one to choose. While this is certainly true in some cases, it's important to consider your opportunity cost. In other words, sometimes a faster delivery pays for itself when you're able to stock your online store and get sales quickly. Waiting several months for inventory to arrive can sometimes mean lost opportunity in the form of lost sales.

DON'T miss the inspection step.

Some business owners choose to fly overseas to inspect their shipment themselves, while others hire an inspection company to do the job for them. No matter which route you take, it's extremely important that your products are inspected before importing them.

Here's just one example of how things can go wrong:

Years ago, we were bringing an order of private labeled artists pallets to various chain stores in the US. Our supplier conducted a thorough report of the shipment before it was exported, and everything looked to be in order.

However, when the shipment arrived we received a phone call from Customs. They had reviewed our paperwork and informed us we were missing the necessary forms or certifications for importing animals.

Animals? We had no idea what they were talking about, and politely informed them that we were not trying to import any animals.

Unbeknownst to us, our supplier in China had stamped PARROTS all over the boxes instead of PALLETS. While Customs found this humorous, and it didn't hurt our company in the long run, we still experienced a slight delay in the delivery of our shipment.

Had we employed a proper inspections agency, or traveled to China to inspect the shipment ourselves, we could have avoided any headaches. Do the inspection!

Importing Checklist

Congratulations! See, that wasn't scary. Mind you, it wasn't sexy either. But the great news is, you've made it this far, which means you're ready to ship your products. Here's a checklist of some of the documents you'll need to have together before your shipment arrives:

- Original Bill of Lading
- Inspection documents
- Certificate of Origin
- Appropriate invoices
- Packing slip
- All the proper certifications for your items

A Final Word...

We started this chapter by stating the obvious: Importing products can feel very overwhelming. This is why we dedicated a huge amount of time in our online training program, The Import Success Formula, to this part of the private label process. We invited our personal customs officials and logistic team to teach and walk through the step by step process so that all our students had a simple, easy to follow, plan for importing with success.

For over three decades, we have been successfully importing products from all over the world. We have seen it all — the good, the bad, and the ugly — and our online course will share it all with you.

With extra input from our incredibly talented international importing team, we go through every step and cover every detail so that you can confidently move forward and import your product like a pro. All of these details are hard to cover in one short chapter, which is why we invite you to check out the full Import Success Formula training.

Phew... Importing is done. Wipe off the sweat from your forehead and let's dive into some creative fun. Join us in the next chapter as we investigate making money on Amazon.

Chapter 6

The Amazon Product Launch Process

Step #5: What A Successful Amazon Launch Looks Like…

You are just about done! Your products are on the way. Time to sit back and wait…

Ugh, no! You thought you has time to breathe before your products arrived from overseas? Nope. Step #5 is all about taking all the work you did and creating a plan of action to share your products with the world.

Customers, make room for "My Perfect Product."

Many entrepreneurs assume that they can't do much until their shipment arrives. Others feel like they just need a break—after all, the journey up to this point has required an incredible amount of time and organizational finesse.

Think about it: You found a perfect product, a perfect supplier, and products are ordered and now being shipped. Now is definitely not the time to sit back and wait.

This period of waiting actually provides a great opportunity to ride the momentum you've built thus far and position your business for quick sales as soon as your inventory arrives. Why take a break now, only to rush a sub-par listing later?

Using the steps outlined in this chapter, you will have all the tools you need to create an optimized listing on Amazon that is ready to publish as soon as your shipment lands. We'll also discuss some other aspects of selling on Amazon that are essential to a successful launch, like how to promote your product, getting customer reviews, some tools that make life on Amazon easier, and much more.

We use Amazon as the online selling platform for this book because of the many benefits Amazon brings. This does not mean you have to *only* use Amazon to sell your products. There are many other additional platforms you can sell your product on and spread awareness of your brand.

Why Amazon?

There are so many benefits of using Amazon as your selling platform, that it's difficult to list them all in one book.

The biggest benefit is the inventory storage that Amazon can provide. Many people do not have access to a warehouse to store inventory. Amazon has you covered, as they have warehouses around the world that charge a minimal fee to store and ship your product to customers.

Amazon also takes care of customer service for you. If customers have issues with the condition of the product when it arrives or the time it takes to receive their orders, Amazon has you covered.

It's almost impossible to get your product into retail brick-and-mortar chains stores, especially if you have no social proof that your product will sell. With Amazon, there is no barrier to entry. Anyone can sell their products, as long as the Amazon guidelines are followed. And you get your products in front of a huge audience! Amazon gives you access to millions of people shopping on their platform.

If all of this wasn't enough reason to launch your products on Amazon, they also give you a business support team. Throughout the launching and selling process, you get their full attention, shipping services, and customer service for your buyers.

Based on experience of owning a warehouse, hiring staff, doing our own shipping and receiving and customer support, we know these things can cost tens of thousands of dollars per month in overhead. Amazon cuts out the large overhead fees that you would pay and makes starting a business easier than ever.

How to Get Started on Amazon

Creating a POWERFUL, kick-butt, optimized product listing.

We won't go into detail of how to set up your Amazon Sellers Central account. If you do need assistance, our online training program, The Import Success Formula covers an in-depth walkthrough for the entire Amazon Seller Central Account Set up.

1. High quality media.

We live in a visual world; use that to your advantage! Generate a handful of high-quality images (1500x1500 pixels) with the samples you received from your supplier. If you private labeled your product and don't have a useable sample, you may need to wait until your inventory arrives to ensure your product photos have your label on them. No matter what route you take, make sure you *never* post blurry or pixelated photos. Making your product look appealing with high quality images is as equally important as having a long list of five-star customer reviews. If your listing is missing either element, your sales are sure to suffer.

2. The power of your listing title.

Create a catchy title that clearly outlines the name and specifications of your product. Be specific. Think of your target audience and what they will type into the Amazon search bar. Use keywords to increase the chances of your product showing up in search results. Think about it: If you were to go to Amazon and try to find your product, what word would you type into the search bar?

3. Choose the right keywords throughout your listing.

The title, five bullet points, and description section should all utilize proper keywords. Merchant Words is a fantastic tool for deciding which keywords will optimize your listing.

You should also look at competitors that are selling similar, or the same, products as you, specifically the ones that have stellar product listings and tons of strong customer reviews. They probably did their research, which you can benefit from.

Take a close look at which words are used repeatedly to hone in on which keywords they're using to optimize their listing. You can use your findings as a starting place when conducting your own keyword research.

4. Maximize your bullet points.

This is the most important part of your product listing. Think about your target audience and use all five bullet points to clearly and persuasively communicate how your product meets their need. Save product details for the next section. What features and **benefits** does your product have? This is where a basic understanding of marketing comes in handy.

Knowing how to use words to capture a shopper's attention is of monumental importance in your bullet points. Where appropriate, you can use capitalization to create a visually appealing list. But be very cautious with this.

Familiarize yourself with Amazon do's and don'ts. Amazon has rules regarding what you can and cannot do in a listing. Even if something is accepted today, keep in mind that Amazon rules are always changing. You don't want Amazon to seize your listing.

5. Detailed description.

As you give a description of your product, don't shy away from the details, and don't worry if the section gets long. Your goal should be to create a description that prospective customers can skim easily while gaining a clear understanding of the benefits of your product.

Do not leave this section as one, long block of text. Break up paragraphs into smaller sections, use bullet points, and make use of capitalization or italics to break up the copy. Be sure to focus on the benefits and give direction on how to complete a purchase. Don't forget to use call-to-action phrases that instruct customers how to buy the product.

6. Create a FNSKU.

Fulfillment Network Stock Keeping Units are the numbers printed directly on your product labels when you're using Fulfillment By Amazon (FBA). FNSKU's identify your items so that the correct product is pulled by Amazon for each sale. If you warehouse and ship yourself, you can skip this step.

7. Stellar customer reviews.

You won't be able to build this part of your listing until after your shipment arrives and you start generating sales, but you can absolutely prepare in advance by letting potential customers know that your product is about to arrive. Maybe create a buzz or take preorders and ship when product arrives.

Look at this time as a pre-launch opportunity. It is important to have a review collection strategy in place. The number of reviews and average star rating is one of the first three things your customers will see, after the title and product photos. We'll talk more about getting customer reviews next.

How Do I Get Customer Reviews?

Prospective customers may *find* your product based on keywords, but they'll *buy* your product based on other people's reviews. So, how do you start getting reviews?

Bottom line? You have to make sales to get reviews. The more sales you make, the more reviews will organically come in. Start with what you have. In other words, reaching out to friends and family can be a convenient way to get your first five reviews published.

You could also create an automated system that will email customers after a sale. The email can really boost customer experience with your company, and it will invite them to write a review.

You could also check out Amazon's Early Reviewer Program, which according to Amazon, "[Encourages] customers who have already purchased a product to share their authentic experience about that product, regardless of whether it is a 1-star or 5-star review."

If you're interested in a program that allows you to give away products in exchange for reviews, also known as incentivized reviews, Amazon Vine is your only option. Back in October 2016, Amazon banned incentivized product reviews for any sellers not using Vine, but this option may be right for you.

Pay Per Click Advertising: Promoting Your Listing

Once your listing is created and saved in draft mode, it's time to start thinking about how you're going to get your listing in front of Amazon shoppers. Promoting your listing through an Amazon pay-per-click (PPC) campaign can be a fantastic way to get your product in front of more people.

PPC campaigns on Amazon are unique because, when a consumer sees your ad, they're not sent somewhere else. They see your ad and click to buy. When using Amazon PPC, the idea is to get your products in front of your potential customer. And Amazon PPC does a great job at that.

Remember, someone on Amazon is there to purchase products, unlike search sites like Google where are doing just that: searching, not purchasing.

How PPC Campaigns Work

Have you ever notices the "sponsored" products section while shopping on Amazon? Sometimes *sponsored products* are on the right side of the page, sometimes they're at the bottom, and sometimes they're mixed in with other listings. Other than the word "sponsored," it looks just like a regular listing.

Every time shoppers conduct a search on Amazon, new *sponsored products* appear because *sponsored products* are actually Amazon PPC ads.

Your specific PPC ad will run off keywords that are relevant to your product, and you get to choose which keywords are featured when you're setting up the campaign. Your ad will show in a customer's search results when they used one or more of those keywords in their search.

Another unique aspect of using PPC advertising has to do with search engine ranking. In a Google search, the vast majority of traffic looks only at the search results on the first page, which is why some companies work tirelessly to optimize their search engine optimization (SEO) ranking.

With Amazon, you can be on the first page by simply paying for it. If you buy a PPC ad and bid high enough, you can be on the first page right away. You just have to be willing to spend as much as it takes to get there.

To promote your product on Amazon, simply take a few

minutes to set up the Amazon pay-per- click (PPC) service in your Seller Account.

It's a quick, intuitive process, but as always, feel free to reach out to us on our private Facebook page with any questions.

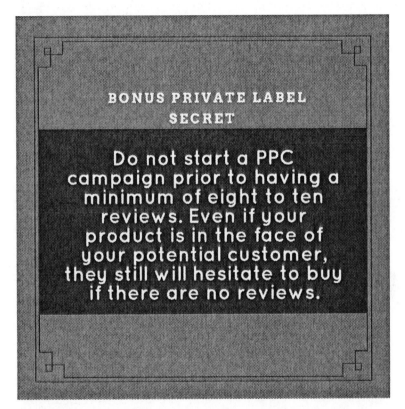

BONUS PRIVATE LABEL SECRET

Do not start a PPC campaign prior to having a minimum of eight to ten reviews. Even if your product is in the face of your potential customer, they still will hesitate to buy if there are no reviews.

Four Tips for Optimizing Your PPC Campaign

1. Monitor the campaign's daily budget and budget cap.

Your *daily budget* represents the upper limit of what you're willing to spend on a specific campaign on a daily basis. By monitoring your campaign throughout the day, you'll avoid the mistake made by many sellers who deplete their budget by afternoon. Many online shoppers buy in the evening. If your daily budget has already been met, you could miss out on valuable business.

The *budget cap* is how much you're willing to spend across all your campaigns. For example, if you create a campaign with a $350 daily budget but your daily cap is $75, a good chunk of that $350 will be significantly underused.

This can ultimately result in poor campaign performance. In short, check your budgets at the end of the day. Even small increases in ad spending can dramatically improve visibility.

2. Monitor your keyword bids.

Amazon allows you to choose the maximum amount you're willing to spend on specific keyword bids when your ad is clicked. People new to Amazon PPC campaigns often cast too wide of a net hoping for quick results and advertise for keywords that aren't relevant to their product.

If you're not getting many impressions on your keyword, there's a chance you're underbidding or not picking the right keyword. If you have a strong number of impressions but few clicks, your keywords—or your product—may not relevant to the customer's search.

3. Monitor negative keywords.

Negative keywords can be powerful if used correctly. For example, if you sell premium products and don't want to be displayed on a search query containing the word "cheap," use negative keywords to narrow the search funnel.

Just don't overdo it with negative keywords, as you may accidentally block the searches where you want your ads to show up.

4. Take advantage of group bids.

Group bids allow you to set a default bid for all the keywords in your ad group. You can still change the individual bids manually, which we recommend, but group bids allow you to take advantage of auctions against competitors when you're not monitoring individual bids.

An Investment for the Future

PPC advertising is a way to invest in your business.

What do we mean?

Every time someone searches a keyword and clicks on your ad, Amazon will start ranking you for that keyword. And every time someone buys your product after clicking on your PPC ad, Amazon will rank you for that keyword again.

Once you get enough sales through ads, you'll start ranking for those keywords organically and will be able to make more sales without ads.

With careful attention to detail, you will be able to achieve amazing sales growth and increased profit.

Brand Registry

Amazon's Brand Registry program is a critical component for any sellers who have manufactured or private labeled a product.

By enrolling your brand and registering yourself as the brand owner, you can better protect your brand by having more control over your listing.

For example, you will be able to:

- Influence the product detail information for your product. As the registered brand owner, the information you submit to the product detail pages for registered products will be displayed automatically, ultimately helping you to specify the correct titles, details, images, and other attributes for the product.

- List the product without its UPC code or EAN number. You'll have an opportunity to specify an alternative key attribute when you list your branded product, instead of just using a standard product ID.

Protect Yourself on Amazon

The following suggestions will keep your listing and account healthy on Amazon. You do not want to make them angry.

1. Analyze the product details in each listing with a fine-tooth comb.

Make sure there is a complete match between the product you sell and the product title, description, bullet points, and keywords. When in doubt, use customer reviews to further hone in on the functionality and/or components of your item.

2. Don't over exaggerate the quality of your product.

Assigning the correct condition to each item you list on Amazon is the first step toward providing a great customer experience. It's important to make a careful assessment of your item before specifying its condition.

Don't list something as "new" and later mention that the item is missing the original box. Use Amazon's Condition Guidelines if you're uncertain how to list your product.

3. Check Amazon's product restriction guidelines.

Unless you know for a fact that you can sell it on Amazon, *don't* sell it. There are dozens of reasons for this, the primary one being that rules change over time. Amazon is constantly updating their policies, and their rules aren't always obvious or logical.

Also, and this may be obvious but still worth mentioning, people on the Internet are sometimes wrong. Don't always trust what you read in online forums, Facebook groups, or blogs. The best way to know what can and can't be listed is to review Amazon's guidelines on restricted products.

4. Make sure you research in the correct product category.

Different product categories have different permissions. For example, products that fall within the *Beauty* or *Health and Personal Care* category on Amazon are heavily monitored. There is a long list of prohibited items, like products containing tinosorb or products containing more than 2% hydroquinone. As a general rule, if your product falls in one of these categories it needs to meet, at minimum, Amazon guidelines.

Where to Send Your Inventory: MFN vs. FBA

Congratulations! Your listing is now ready to launch once your product arrives. However, you have one more big decision to make before that happens: Where are you going to store your product, and what are your plans for order fulfillment?

Choosing Fulfillment by Amazon (FBA) means that you'll ship your product directly to an Amazon FBA warehouse, and Amazon will ship items directly from the warehouse to your customers. This means that you don't have to worry about renting a warehouse to store your products. Amazon will warehouse them for you.

One of the biggest advantages of FBA is that your Prime customers will be able to take advantage of free shipping. Since they're already paying for their annual Prime membership, they are less likely to purchase something that has a mandatory shipping cost, which you see in merchant fulfillment.

Amazon also takes care of the customer service for all FBA products. And did we mention that Amazon has incredibly low shipping rates that you will have a hard time competing with? Take advantage of that!

Choosing a Merchant Fulfillment Network (MFN) means products will be stored at your home, place of business, or warehouse, and you will ship them directly to customers to fulfill orders. You'll need to ensure that all product, packaging, and labeling details are exactly as you ordered them, and meet the exact specifications required by Amazon.

One huge advantage of choosing to store items and fulfill orders yourself is you won't be charged FBA fees. Amazon charges per cubic foot of warehouse space used each month, and additional fees apply for items that sit on shelves for extended periods of time before being shipped to customers. This makes FBA costly for long-tail items that may sit around for a while before they are purchased.

Companies have their own reasoning for either using FBA or maintaining their own inventory and shipping products personally.

For example, using FBA for your fulfillment channel can be great if you just want to set things up and forget about them or don't have access or the resources to a warehouse. Instead of managing orders yourself or maintaining the inventory, you have access to one of the greatest warehouse and distribution networks in the world: Amazon.

On the other hand, fulfilling your own products presents several opportunities not found with FBA, like personalizing product packaging—and potentially ensuring fewer returns because of items damaged during shipping, branding your company apart from Amazon to build better brand loyalty among customers, providing added customer service, and being able to better monitor reviews for fraudulent activity. And now with Seller Fulfilled Prime, your customers too can access two-day shipping directly from you.

FBA Warehouse Locations

According to MWPVL International, as of December 2016, Amazon has almost one hundred fulfillment and redistribution centers in North America, including six in Canada and one just outside Mexico City.

It's Time to Launch!

We are so proud of you! Launching your listing on Amazon is a thrilling experience. It's wonderful to watch the hard work you've put in start to pay off as the sales start rolling in. There's no doubt that selling physical products is an exciting, thriving industry to be a part of right now. In the last five years alone, online marketplaces have completely redefined how billions of people shop for their everyday needs.

For anyone with an enterprising spirit, there is not only great potential to make it as a business owner, there is actually potential for you to make it BIG. Success doesn't happen overnight, but with careful research, preparation, commitment to the process, and more time with resources like this book, you can master private labeling and start making the income you deserve.

And the best part? The momentum doesn't end with your Amazon launch. There's a big world of opportunity out there for private labelers. Want to see how you can add even more income to your business with the same product you just launched? All right, let's move on to the next chapter.

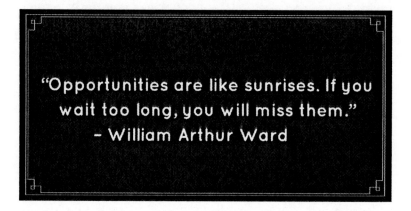

"Opportunities are like sunrises. If you wait too long, you will miss them."
– William Arthur Ward

Chapter 7

Beyond Amazon

Online retail is simply a stepping stone to a bigger world for your brand. We want to help you create a business that can not only survive, but also thrive beyond an Amazon listing. Creating a private label business is all about building a brand that can be launched and showcased in retail stores and around the world.

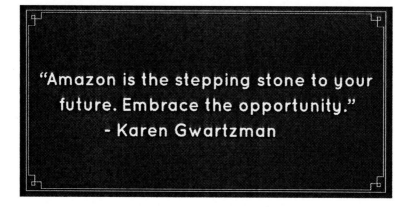

"Amazon is the stepping stone to your future. Embrace the opportunity."
- Karen Gwartzman

Retailers around the world are constantly looking for successful brands to add to their shelves, giving you an incredible opportunity to expose your items to even more shoppers. Just take one of our former PLU students as an example:

A few months into her launch on Amazon, Kim's sales were not what she expected. Feeling like she had tried everything, Kim was frustrated by the lack of improvement. She reached out to the Private Label University for help.

Through personalized, one-on-one coaching, and a quick trip with us to our Live China event, her brand started attracting more customers. She made adjustments to her packaging and product design, spent many careful hours optimizing her Amazon listing, and found better suppliers that provided her with better pricing and quality. Kim worked hard, and within a few short months, her sales showed huge improvement. In fact, they quadrupled.

Kim was killing it on Amazon and wanted more! We began helping her think about life beyond Amazon. We taught her how to cast a wider net so she could get her product into the hands of every shopper. With careful study and attention to detail, Kim took her business to a whole new level.

Today, Kim is still selling on Amazon, but her brand is also featured on four other online sites and in retail chain stores across the country. She saw the opportunity beyond Amazon and jumped on it—and has been reaping the benefits ever since.

Selling your product in retail stores across the country may seem like a giant leap from where you're at now, but what if, in a few months or years you hit a ceiling with Amazon and start dreaming about life beyond an online marketplace?

Alternatively, what if the day comes when Amazon closes its doors? If your entire business revolves around selling on Amazon, you would run the risk of losing everything.

These are just some of the reasons we encourage all of our budding entrepreneurs to **dream big** and **cast a wide net**. Although the world of online retail is burgeoning and shows no signs of slowing down, brick-and-mortar retail is not going anywhere. What an opportunity to spread your brand and build a sustainable, profitable business.

Why Put Your Brand in Retail Stores?

We're living in an age when private label brands are experiencing tremendous success. So much success, in fact, that it can be hard to remember that in the not-so-distant past consumers made their purchasing decisions based almost entirely on loyalty to name-brand products.

The perception of private label brands used to be quite negative. In North America, shoppers felt that private label brands were for people on tight budgets that couldn't afford the best.

Consumers were fiercely brand-loyal, and in most categories, popular name brands were king. Whether it was Huggies diapers for the kids, Heinz ketchup for summer barbecues, or Sears appliances throughout the house, consumers bought products that were well known, established brands.

What changed? The economic recession in the early 2000s and the global meltdown in 2008 completely shifted the retail landscape. Driven by lower prices, consumers started consistently looking for the biggest bang for their buck.

And for the first time in retail history, this trend was consistent across almost every single product category.

For example, one survey from late 2010 indicated that 93% of consumers had changed their grocery shopping habits because of the economic downturn, and many of them did so by trying out more private label brands, sampling everything from hand soap to frozen pizza.

Even though the economy has started to stabilize in the last few years, consumers grew accustomed to saving money by turning away from big name brands. It's how they saved money throughout the recession, and the preference to buy low does not show signs of slowing.

EXTRA SPECIAL SECRET - SHHHH...

Many products that are private labeled today are the same products made by the same manufacturers that make the brand-name products.

Plus, private labelers have done a remarkable job of increasing in the quality of their products in the last ten years. Research shows consumers feel that, in terms of quality and value, these products are as good as the name brands they used to purchase.

What does this mean for you, the online seller? It's clear that the door that was first opened by economic necessity won't close anytime soon. Private label brands are no longer viewed as low-cost alternatives to name brands; shoppers are genuinely excited about high-quality products that fulfill their needs across a variety of price points.

What's more, fewer shoppers assume big name brand products equate to top quality. That same survey from 2010 showed that 57% of consumers agreed with the statement, *"Brand names are not better quality."* More recently, that figure inched up to 64%.

Private labeling, both for online shopping and for brick-and-mortar stores, has made its mark as a viable business model in the retail world. Because studies show that consumers have gotten used to saving money, your private label business has the potential to not only make it, but also make it BIG.

Four Tips for Private Labelers Entering Retail

Putting your brand on the shelves at retail stores can open doors that you've never dreamed possible for you and your family. Here are a few tips to help you along the way:

1. Packaging & Labeling Considerations.

The packaging and design of a product are always important, especially when your private label agreement is with a retailer. You may find it prudent to offer a display of what your product can do for retailers.

If you have a consumer product, take time to package your product so it sells itself. You could also provide a diagram of what complementary products yours should be displayed next to on retail shelves.

2. Understand the Competition.

Retailers typically bring private label brands to their shelves for competitive reasons. To sell the concept effectively, you should know your target retailer's competitors and how your product will increase their competitive edge.

When you approach a company with a private label proposal, show them how and why their target customers need—and will ultimately love—your product. Try using surveys or interviews with potential customers to help reinforce your point.

3. Keep the Quality High.

Thirty years ago, there was a distinct gap quality between private label and national brand product. By *national brand* we mean those incredibly well-known name brands you see throughout stores in the United States, like Q-Tip cotton swabs, Kleenex tissues, and Campbell's soup.

Today, that quality gap has narrowed to the point that private label brands now have consistently high quality across product categories, making them serious competitors for national brands.

This is good news for private labelers because the more high-quality private label products are on the shelves, the more readily consumers will choose those products over the higher-priced name brands.

Even so, make sure you don't skimp on product improvements for your brand.

This helps enhance your brand's perceived superiority, provides the basis for informative and provocative advertising, increases the brand's sustainable price premium over the competition, and raises the costs to private label imitators who are constantly forced to play catch-up.

4. Consider Developing a Premium Line.

Several innovative retailers in North America have shown the rest of the private label world how to develop a private label line that delivers quality superior to that of national brands. You can learn a lot from the example they've set.

Let's look at President's Choice as an example. Parent company Loblaw, which has thousands of grocery stores across the country, has developed this premium private label brand of 1,500 items, which includes the leading chocolate-chip cookie sold in Canada.

As a result of careful, worldwide procurement, Loblaw has squeezed Canada's national brands between its top-of-the-line President's Choice label and their regular Loblaw private label line. And President's Choice has even expanded beyond Loblaws' store boundaries — fifteen grocery chains in the States now sell President's Choice products as a premium private label line.

The wonderful benefit of owning a private label brand business, whether your brand is sold online or in a brick and mortar business, is that you have total control of what you want to do with it.

We've had students who had a ton of success with their brand, only to be approached by companies wanting to buy their business or brand.

Yes, you read that correctly; you can sell your brand or business even if you are just an Amazon business. Many of our students have sold or are in the process of selling their Amazon business.

Selling Your Private Label Business

Do you view your company as an asset? Did you know that dozens of online businesses are sold every day? Retail chain stores, entrepreneurs, venture capitalists, and other retail marketplaces constantly look at brands on Amazon that are creating a buzz. Brands that have only had a presence on Amazon for twelve months are being purchased every week.

Even if you don't plan on selling your company, you never know when your situation might change. Knowing how much your business is worth is another aspect of thinking about life beyond Amazon. Just take one of our former clients, Samuel, as an example of what is possible:

Samuel launched his Amazon business with two products. He spent his first year meticulously building his brand, paid attention to customer experience and prioritized getting strong reviews, and listened to customer feedback.

Using everything he learned, he made updates to the product packaging to improve customer experience. As the months progressed, his brand gained popularity on Amazon and the "bigger fish" started to notice.

Eighteen months after his launch, Samuel sold his business for over $300,000.

Your private label business can be an attractive investment for the right person—for example, someone who feels they don't have the skills, knowledge, or time to start their own company.

If your business is a well-oiled, profitable machine that is chugging along nicely, you may be surprised to learn how much your company is worth.

How Much is Your Business Worth?

The value of your business is in its ability to produce profit. The amount a buyer is willing to pay will all come down to the company's return-on-investment (ROI) and relative risk. The lower the risk, the higher the price and vice-versa. Here is a popular formula used to determine valuation:

Valuation = (Monthly Net Profit x Multiple) + Inventory At Cost

When determining your **Monthly Net Profit**, try using a twelve-month average. Sometimes a three- or six-month average can be used when the business is in a high-growth phase, but only if it's indicative of a realistic view of the future.

Remember, the average needs to be extrapolated from what a buyer would expect to make on a monthly basis going forward, and only things that are absolutely required to maintain your business will be taken out of your monthly net profit as expenses. As an example, business trips to China.

If your business is less than a year old, you may still be able to sell your business.

If you're considering selling your Amazon business, or simply want to know the value of your company, there are plenty of resources out there that can help you. A quick Google search is a great place to start.

5 Tips to Maximize the Value of Your Amazon Business

Once you've determined the value of your company, it's time to put on your strategic-thinking hat. You want your business to be worth more right? Whether you are looking to sell or not, this is important information for any business owner.

1. **Maintain updated, detailed financials.** You always want to show potential buyers a complete picture of your cash flow through your income and cash flow statements. Also, keep in mind that a buyer won't necessarily want to sift through months of records to get the big picture, so be ready to make trends and growth patterns apparent. You could also keep an updated prospectus, which is a twenty- to thirty-page document that describes your business to potential buyers.

2. **Create a separate company.** If you are thinking of selling your business at some point, or you at least want to leave that option open, set up a separate limited liability company (LLC) or corporation and create a separate bank account.

3. **Diversify your product offering.** A company that receives 80% of its profit from one product carries significantly more risk than a company that has a diversified offering. When you're thinking big picture, you'll want to plan for multiple SKU's, multiple suppliers, multiple traffic and sales channels, and also target multiple keywords. Potential buyers could see risk if you only have a single SKU's, one supplier, or are only selling in one marketplace.

4. **Document all of your systems and processes, and update these files as your business grows.** This can help save an incredible amount of time later on if you actually decide you want to sell. You will have to train your buyer as you hand over the

business, so be sure to keep detailed records of how to keep your well-oiled machine purring smoothly. Luckily for you, private label businesses are some of the easiest businesses to understand and train a new buyer on.

5. **Sharpen your brand.** Have a very clear representation of who you are as a brand reflected everywhere – in your design, copy, blog and all media, such as images, video, etc. Ensure that your brand messaging is consistent across platforms. And remember, the more you can show who your target customer is and how your brand appeals to them, the less work a new owner will have to do.

Who Will Buy Your Amazon Business?

There are, of course, many different types of investors interested in buying private label companies. Here are three main classifications we've seen:

The Corporate Guru: This is someone looking to buy his or her first business. They are often a high-paid employee or C-level executive with disposable cash, IRA, savings, or access to an SBA loan.

The Internet Entrepreneur: These are individuals who have typically been in the industry for a while and have a good understanding of what it takes to run an online business. They are either fresh off the sale of their last business or looking to add another business to their portfolio.

The Brick-and-Mortar Entrepreneur: These are brick-and-mortar store owners who are looking for a move into the online retail world. Because they've already started a retail business, they want to acquire something that they don't have to start from scratch again.

Selling your company may not be a part of your big picture plan right now, but as we've said, you never know where life will take you. Being mindful of what makes a business valuable can only help you as you move forward.

The Bigger Picture

We meet a lot of sellers who only have their sights set on Amazon, but as this chapter has explained, private label brands are in the midst of a major retail transformation. This is creating incredible opportunities for private label businesses.

Does the thought of building a sustainable business that has unlimited growth potential make you want to get out of bed in the morning? If so, maybe you resonated with Kim's story at the beginning of this chapter. Maybe you felt a flutter of excitement at the thought of expanding your brand into retail chain stores across the country.

Or perhaps you resonated more with Samuel's story. We meet many entrepreneurs who are always on the lookout for the next big profitable opportunity. These types of people are often drawn to the private label opportunity because, when it's done properly, a successful private label business can be flipped for a profit in no time.

If you've never thought about life beyond Amazon, we hope this chapter has made you curious about dreaming BIGGER!

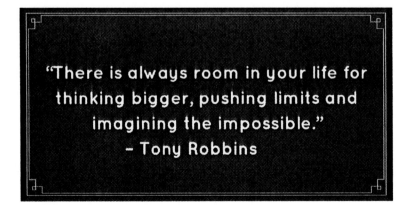

"There is always room in your life for thinking bigger, pushing limits and imagining the impossible."
– Tony Robbins

Opportunity is right in front of you… Take the Leap!

You did it! You made it to the end of the book. Our goal was to show you how easy it is to find a product, brand it as your own and share it with the world. We really wanted to share our stories, experience and process with you so you can see how easy it is to add a product to your existing business or start a business with products.

In the limited time we've had together, we have covered a lot of information. We gave you all the steps, shared our experience, and gave you tips from others who have made this journey, too.

Through all of this, we hope you'll take away the many benefits of private labeling. We wanted you to see that anyone can do it; it's now up to you to just start…

We are waiting on the other side for you. Take the leap. The grass is green over here. Whether you're hoping to add a private label product to your business, build a business around products that help attract clients, build a global brand or just make more money, we're here to help.

We wrote this book for you. If you found value within these pages, please don't keep us a secret. You can head over to Amazon and leave a review that will help others make the leap, too.

Programs and Products

Are You Ready to Take Action?

How to get started...

1. 5-Day FREE Private Label Bootcamp – Join Karen and Neil as they walk through the 5-step process to private labeling in their fast track to private labeling boot camp.

   This 5-day training is packed with a ton of value. And, nuggets that were not shared in the book.

2. The Import Success Formula – 50+ training videos that walk you through the entire private label process from start to launch.

   Nothing is left to the imagination, they cover EVERYTHING! Check out the bonuses and private mentoring call with Karen and Neil. The goal is to see you succeed.

3. VIP LIVE China Event – The fastest way to get started and see results. Personal training with Karen, Neil and the PLU team in China. Up close and personal.

This is the VIP of private Labeling where Karen and Neil teach you 3 decades of skills and strategies and HOW TO IMPLEMENT THEM with them by your side.

This event is for those who are ready to take action and implement all in 7 days. This event will leave you with 100% success in finding a product, supplier and samples all within a few days so that you can start making money fast.

4. Private 1:1 coaching – Due to its popularity and limited space, an interview is required.

5. Not sure which program is right for you or you have questions? No worries. Set up a time to chat and let's brainstorm some ideas.

Important Links

Play along and win a prize:
http://privatelabelu.com/book-code/

Join our LIVE China event:
http://bit.ly/PLUChina

Read some testimonials
http://bit.ly/PLUtestimonial

Join the PLU Bootcamp
http://bit.ly/PLUbootcamp

Sign up for 1:1 coaching:
http://bit.ly/plucoaching

Private Label University chat:
http://bit.ly/PLUchat

Access the Import Success Formula
www.importsuccessformula.com/program

Join the private Facebook group
www.facebook.com/groups/PrivateLabelUniversity/

Email the authors:
info@privatelabeluniversity.com

Leave a review on Amazon:
http://amzn.to/2sr4oi3

Gwartzman

About the Authors

Karen and Neil Gwartzman, creators of the Private Label University®, have over 35 years of experience private labeling products. They have sold millions of dollars of products in retail stores across North America and on multiple online marketplaces including Amazon and Ebay. Serial entrepreneurs and international speakers, they have mastered and bottled the 5-step process to private labeling, and have personally guided countless chain stores and entrepreneurs into building successful private label businesses.

The Private Label University® is a place for like-minded entrepreneurs who are ready to build a thriving global brand. PLU students enjoy the benefits of reaching millions of customers worldwide as the Gwartzmans walk them through their proven 5-step process, coaching them through all the nuances of sourcing, importing, and private labeling.

Gwartzman

About Neil Gwartzman

The son of a manufacturing, distribution and retail pioneer in Canada, Neil has been bringing ideas to life since he was just ten years old. A visionary who conducted business in more than ten countries around the world before the age of 30, Neil has uncovered the hidden secrets of product sourcing, manufacturing, importing, and sales — in both online marketplaces and retail store shelves — so much so that his colleagues refer to him as the Industry-Wide Powerhouse!

Having played a critical role in the rise of countless successful companies over the past 30 years, Neil has identified the key steps required to sell millions of dollars in products worldwide. Privileged to have worked under some of the most influential masters in the industry, Neil has honed his skills as an ambassador for entrepreneurs, and international speaker, serving today as the missing link between the those that want to sell products and the customers that will buy them. Today his client list includes some of the largest retail stores in the world, along with hundreds of entrepreneurs just like you. And of course, Neil still continues to work in the trenches as he builds his own private label businesses.

When he's not breaking down barriers for the next big thing, Neil is at home in Colorado enjoying time with his beautiful wife and business partner Karen, their two children, and three enormous dogs.

Gwartzman

About Karen Gwartzman

The daughter of an entrepreneur that helped build a pharmaceutical franchise in Canada, Karen was born into the entrepreneurial world. Nicknamed *the dreamer* by family and friends, Karen has been building businesses in just about every industry you can imagine, from fashion to health care, for more than 25 years.

Karen started private labeling products 16 years ago, shortly after moving to the States with Neil and their two children. Due to licensing restrictions, she could no longer work as a dental hygienist, She took on the most important job in the world: raising their kids. Unfortunately, this new job didn't pay well, so Karen reached out to her husband for guidance in starting her first private labeling business. She has never once looked back!

When she started, Karen knew nothing about sourcing, importing, and selling products. She believes if she could figure out how to launch a successful international business in the physical product industry, anyone at any stage of life could do the same. This belief deepened as she taught her two children how to private label products and launch their own businesses.

When she is not developing private label products, growing her business globally, or giving back to support Big Dogs, Karen stays busy raising her two incredible young dreamers, traveling with Neil, and enjoying the bond they have with their three furry companions.

Gwartzman

Glossary of Terms & Acronyms

A

Anti-Dumping Tariff: dumping occurs when a company exports a product at a price lower than the price it normally charges in its own home market. Anti-dumping tariffs are imposed by domestic government on foreign imports that it believes are priced below fair market value.

ASIN: *Amazon Standard Identification Number.* This is given to every product you list on Amazon. Usually in the format B00xxxxxxx, an ASIN is attached to the listing, not the product itself. No two items will ever have the same ASIN (even when the same product is listed multiple times). You can use this number when searching for a product on Amazon.

ATOP: *At Time Of Posting.* We typically see this used in forums or Facebook groups when someone is getting the word out on a hot new deal, for example, *"ATOP I found this product for $8 each at Target."*

AWB: *Air Waybill.* A document used when shipping via air; ensures that the correct goods are delivered to you. The air waybill is provided by your airline or air freight forwarder. It acts as a receipt for your supplier, as it proves that your inventory has been sent.

B

BB seller: *Buy Box Seller.* The person whose listing is shown when a customer is looking for products online.

Bill of Lading: similar to an AWB, this document is for sea freight and signifies that the goods described have been loaded on board the ship.

BOLO: *Be On Look Out.* Many sellers use this for items that are sold out online but may still be available in stores locally.

Bonds: a contract that guarantees the payment of import duties and taxes.

Brand registry: a program offered by Amazon for sellers who manufacture their own brand of products, giving them total control of their listing.

BSR: *Best Sellers Rank.* Items on Amazon are ranked according to their sales volume and category.

Buy Box: the actual listing that a buyer sees of the product they want to purchase.

C

CCC: *CamelCamelCamel.com* allows you to see the price and rank history of a product when you're working on sourcing products online.

CFR or C&F: *Cost and Freight.* A quote that does *not* include insurance. The supplier's liability ends once the goods are delivered to the carrier, whether by sea or air.

CIF: *Cost Insurance and Freight.* The quoted cost of door-to-door delivery, from the factory or warehouse of your supplier to you, and this particular quote includes insurance.

COGS: *Cost Of Goods Sold.*

Consignee: the owner or purchaser of the goods; the financially responsible party. Also referred to as the *Importer of Record.*

COO: *Country of Origin.* An important domestic regulation mandates that your product show the country where the it originated.

Copyrights: an official government registration that protects the expression of ideas, for example, all creative or artistic work.

Customs Broker: handles the importing of your product.

D

Deemed Value: an amount calculated by Customs in some countries to determine the value of the goods for duty and tax purposes.

E

EAN: *European Article Number.* If you sell in Europe, your products will be assigned this 13-digit code, also called an International Article Number (IAN).

EX Works: outlines the price of purchasing a product directly from the factory. Any shipping fees or duties are typically not included in this quote.

F

FBM or **MFN**: *Fulfillment by Merchant* or *Merchant Fulfilled Network*. This means the merchant is responsible for picking, packing, and shipping the products, as well as providing customer support for the product.

FCL: *Full Container Load.* When your sea shipment fills a container.

FITCA: *Federal Import Trade Compliance Agency.*

FNSKU: *Fulfillment Network Stock Keeping Unit.* These are the numbers printed directly on your product labels when you use FBA. FNSKUs identify your items so that the correct product is pulled for each sale.

FOB: *Freight On Board* or *Free on Board.* This means all freight charges to the point of loading have been included in the quoted price. If you receive an *FOB*, ask what freight and other charges will be involved in transporting your shipment to the air/sea port.

FTL: *Full Truckload.* When your freight shipment fills an entire truck.

Freight Agent: moves your freight around, either to you or another supplier.

Freight Forwarder: facilitates the forwarding of shipments from the port to your receiving destination.

G

Gated category or **Restricted category:** products being sold on Amazon are monitored. Some categories, like healthcare & beauty, are restricted to ensure the health and safety of Amazon customers.

GTIN: *Global Trade Identification Numbers.* These are universal identifiers used around the world to find product information across databases.

H

HBA: *Health & Beauty Aids.* Refers to a category on Amazon.

HTF: *Hard To Find.* These products often result in higher prices on Amazon.

I

IL: *Inventory Lab.* A popular company that offers inventory management and listing on Amazon.

ISF: *Importer Security Filing.* A document that must be electronically submitted to Customs when your cargo is arriving into the US via sea freight.

L

LCL: *Less than Container Load.* When your sea shipment does not fill an entire container.

Lightning deals: a promotion in which a limited number of discounts are offered on an item for a short period of time.

LTL: *Less than Truckload.* When your freight shipment does not fill an entire truck.

M

MAP: *Minimum Advertised Price.* A price agreement between suppliers and retailers stating the lowest price for an item to be advertised. Relevant when buying wholesale or direct from a manufacturer.

MOQ: *Minimum Order Quantity.* The smallest amount a supplier requires you to order.

P

Patent: an official government registration that protects your invention.

Perfect Product Syndrome (PPS): a term we use at the Private Label University to describe the frustration many entrepreneurs feel while searching for new product ideas.

PPC: *Pay Per Click.* An advertising service provided by Amazon for Amazon sellers to help them promote their product listing.

Pro Forma Invoice: an invoice that confirms all the specifications of your order, sent to you by the supplier before you officially place the order. Not the same as a commercial invoice, which you'll need to ask for separately to ensure your shipment clears customs.

R

Replen refers to a replenishable item, an item that can be purchased and sold repeatedly, usually from the same supplier.

S

SC: *Seller Central.* Your main dashboard when logged into your Amazon Seller Account.

Schedule Rates: a rate chart published by the carrier. In the case of postal services, it is not subject to negotiation and you will always pay that rate. In the case of commercial carriers, it is the absolute maximum rate, which can usually be negotiated.

Scouting: looking for products to resell online.

SKU: *Stock Keeping Unit.* The numbers printed directly on your labels. They identify your items so that the correct product is pulled for each sale.

T

Tariff/Tariff Codes: the taxes or duties to be paid on a particular class of imports or exports.

TIA: *Thanks In Advance.* You'll find this in online forums or discussion groups. When someone asks a question, they'll end with TIA, as if to say *thank you for any answers you may provide*.

Trademark: a word, phrase, logo, design, or company name that identifies and distinguishes the goods of one business from the goods of businesses.

U

Unique Signature Formula® **(USF):** a formula we've developed at the Private Label University to help sellers create a thriving, profitable online business.

UPC: *Universal Product Code.* A 12-digit barcode that can be found on almost all products in the retail world.

USPTO: *US Patent and Trademark Office.* The official government agency that is the only place to get federally registered patents and trademarks.

W

WL: *White Labeling,* also referred to as *Private Labeling.* Involves purchasing an item from a manufacturer, applying your own brand, and reselling the product.